The Fruit of Christ's Presence |||

D1301929

# THE
# FRUIT
# = OF =
# CHRIST'S
# PRESENCE

## HARRY L. POE

**BROADMAN PRESS**
NASHVILLE, TENNESSEE

© Copyright 1990 ● Broadman Press
All Rights Reserved
4260-12
ISBN: 0-8054-6012-8
Dewey Decimal Classification: 248
Subject Headings: SPIRITUAL LIFE // HOLY SPIRIT
Library of Congress Catalog Number: 89-38433
Printed in the United States of America

Unless otherwise noted, all Scripture quotations are from the *Revised Standard Version of the Bible*, copyrighted 1946, 1952, © 1971, 1973.

Scripture quotations marked (KJV) are from the King James Version of the Bible.

**Library of Congress Cataloging-in-Publication Data**

Poe, Harry Lee, 1950-
    The fruit of Christ's presence / Harry L. Poe.
        p. cm.
    ISBN 0-8054-6012-8
        1. Fruit of the Spirit. 2. Spiritual life--Baptist authors.
    I. Title.
    BV4501.2.P55543 1990
        234'.13--dc20

89-38433
CIP

||| For Mary Anne |||

# ||| Contents |||

# 1 ||| Spiritual Horticulture

Oliver began coming to the chapel as soon as he arrived at prison. In the years I knew him there, I saw him grow in spiritual maturity "from glory unto glory." But Oliver remembered his life before Jesus Christ entered it. He feared that he might lapse back into the life of alcohol, drugs, and sex that had once gripped him.

Oliver recognized his weaknesses, and he wondered if he could truly be a Christian when he still had such temptations. He feared that the presence of such strong temptations meant that he was not truly saved. Oliver is not the only Christian that struggles with the temptation to sin. Many Christians hold secret inner fears and doubts about their relationship to the Lord because of the tremendous struggle they have with temptations.

## The Struggle with Sin

Like many other Christians, Oliver feared that temptation proved God had abandoned him. Since I had seen the power of God in Oliver's life, my first impulse was to laugh at such a silly fear. But he keenly felt the spiritual struggle within him, and he did not know how to fight it. His fear of temptation so consumed his mind that the very struggle to overcome it made it even stronger.

In Galatians, Paul talks about the struggle that Christians face between the flesh and the Spirit. The passions and desires of the flesh are opposed to the desires of the Spirit. Each has its own agenda and goals, and they are contrary to one another. Non-Christians do not have to contend with the same kind of struggle because the struggle grows out of the presence of the Holy Spirit in a person's life. While everyone has struggles of conscience, which are a dimension of the human spirit, only Christians experience the warfare of the flesh and the Spirit of God.

I asked Oliver if his drinking and carousing had bothered him before he submitted his life to Jesus Christ. "No," he said. In fact, he had enjoyed it a lot! Now that he was a Christian, though, he was miserable.

"Rejoice, then, Oliver," I told him. "Only God can make sin seem miserable. Your struggle proves that God is at work in your life."

Oliver thought that his struggle with sin proved that God was not with him. Many Christians labor under this same dread. Part of the reason probably stems from the fact that many Christians do not understand the idea of sanctification. So much has been said about salvation as eternal life that many Christians do not know what God does with us before heaven. Spiritual growth as a dimension of salvation equal in importance with justification has never found a place in the understanding of many Christians.

When the struggle against sin comes, Christians often feel such shame that they tell no one else about it. They feel alone and isolated, as though they are the only ones who have gone through such a battle. They feel they have failed the Lord and the church. Instead of drawing closer into the fellowship of the church for support and encouragement, they may retreat or drop out of church altogether. Sin carries with it a sense of shame and guilt that some Christians even feel sinful in the temptation. At times like this, the priesthood of Christ has special significance: "For because he himself has suffered and been tempted, he is able to help those who are tempted" (Heb. 2:18).

One of the most alienating factors in our struggle with sin is the fear that others will not understand what we go through. This fear is accompanied by another fear—that we will be rejected because of our weaknesses. Because of His human experience, however, Christ offers us an understanding heart that we cannot find anywhere else, even from ourselves:

> For we have not a high priest who is unable to sympathize with our weaknesses, but one who in every respect has been tempted as we are, yet without sin. Let us then with confidence draw near to the throne of grace, that we may receive mercy and find grace to help in time of need (Heb. 4:15-16).

Christ stands ready to help, but too often we do not seek His help and battle it out alone with our own self-condemnation for company.

I have never been tempted by alcohol or drugs. In all likelihood I will live out my life, and these will never threaten me. The idea of sticking a needle in my arm for fun is positively crazy to me. I have had a horror of needles since I was a small child and had to go to the county health department for polio shots. Oliver, on the other hand, does not have the load of little fears that keep me from experimenting with new and daring experiences.

Oliver thinks his temptations are the worst of all temptations, primarily because they are his. He does not struggle with temptations like pride, arrogance, envy, gossip, and jealousy. To him these temptations are too small to be given honorable mention. They have no power over him. He does not take them seriously. But they are monsters that threaten to devour me.

Every Christian has his or her own set of temptations to sin. When Paul mentions the works of the flesh in Galatians 5:19-21, he does not give an exhaustive list. His examples, and things like them (v. 21), comprise the work of the flesh. To Paul's brief list in Galatians we could add Colossians 3:5-8 or 2 Timothy 3:2-4. None of these are exhaustive. They simply illustrate the variety of forms which passion and desire can promote. While the average church member may not be tempted by fornication and drunkenness, many churches face the problem of enmity, strife, and party spirit within the body. Works of the flesh, then, are any habits or attitudes that stand in opposition to the Spirit of God.

Oliver's greatest blessing and hope lay in his willingness to confess his spiritual weakness. He recognized the sinfulness of the desires that captivated him. Without a willingness to confess or acknowledge a problem, a solution to the problem will never occur. People who are comfortable with their weaknesses see no need to resist the temptation to gratify every weakness.

I once knew a church member who felt sorry for himself for years. He compounded the problem by convincing himself that the people of the church and community did not like him, wanted to hurt him, talked about him, or deliberately avoided him. The more the man pouted, the more he imagined he had been treated badly. He responded by gossiping about other people and picking fights. He loved to feel sorry for himself! It was a passion which the church member had devoted his life to gratifying. And he would never confess the sinfulness of it, though it had created a wall between him and other believers.

## The Beginning of Growth

Spiritual growth and maturity will only take place when a Christian yearns to follow the impulses of the Holy Spirit. Part of that desire involves a willingness to be taught by the Spirit. Jesus said that when the Spirit came, He would convince the world of sin and righteousness (John 16:8), as well as teach believers all things (John 14:26). Spiritual growth is not inevitable, though it is the will of God for which He has made provision.

### Christ: The Goal of Growth

Over and over the New Testament laments Christians who remain babes after the new birth instead of growing to maturity (Heb. 5:11-14; 1 Cor. 3:1-3). Christlikeness is the goal of spiritual maturity. The aim of the new birth is nothing short of producing offspring for God who conform to the image of Christ (Eph. 4:13-14; Gal. 4:19). Until Christians are truly Christlike, they still require spiritual growth and maturity. God's purpose is that Christians should be "chips off the old block" so that their lineage is unmistakably "like father, like son." As Christ bears the image of the Father, so Christians are to bear the image of the Son.

Instead of focusing on Christ and being like Him, however, many Christians like Oliver try to grow simply by battling sin and temptation. When the Galatians struggled with the questions of spiritual growth, Paul asked them the question: "Having begun with the Spirit, are you now ending with the flesh?" (Gal. 3:3). Spiritual growth is primarily a work of the Holy Spirit; therefore, anyone desiring to be like Christ must depend upon the Holy Spirit to produce the transformation. The Holy Spirit produces the transformation of regeneration that Jesus described to Nicodemus (John 3:6-7), and the Holy Spirit also produces the transformation in holiness that we call spiritual growth.

Spiritual growth, then, is not something a Christian is supposed to do or make happen. On the contrary, a Christian's role in spiritual growth is being a willing vessel in which the Lord works. Paul expresses it this way:

Now the Lord is the Spirit, and where the Spirit of the Lord is, there is freedom. And we all, with unveiled face, beholding the glory of the

Lord, are being changed into his likeness from one degree of glory to another; for this comes from the Lord who is the Spirit (2 Cor. 3:17-18).

Victory over sin does not come in fighting sin but in being close to the Lord, who banishes sin by His glorious presence.

## The Fruit of the Spirit

In contrast to the works of the flesh, Paul speaks of transformed Christian life as the fruit of the Spirit (Gal. 5:22-23). The Spirit may give many gifts, but it only produces one fruit. Paul says, "The fruit of the Spirit is . . . ." and then gives nine qualities to describe that fruit. The fruit of an apple tree may be described as round, sweet, juicy, red, crisp, firm, and tart. Each quality represents a different dimension of the fruit. All dimensions are important, but there is still only one fruit. The Spirit does not produce one kind of fruit in one Christian and another kind of fruit in another Christian. While every soul is unique and each personality respected, the Spirit is producing Christlike beings. The qualities that describe the fruit of the Spirit are the same qualities that describe "the Lord who is the Spirit."

In the Galatians passage, Paul used nine characteristics to describe the fruit of the Spirit. The *Revised Standard Version* renders these characteristics as love, joy, peace, patience, kindness, goodness, faithfulness, gentleness, and self-control. The *King James Version* renders them as love, joy, peace, long-suffering, gentleness, goodness, faith, meekness, and temperance. The different words chosen by the translators give insight into the meaning of the Greek words Paul used to describe the quality of a Spirit-filled life. The terms appear in other places, and these passages indicate how highly the New Testament church regarded these qualities as characteristic of a life in Christ. While the terms are often found by themselves, the frequency with which they are grouped together illustrates their interdependency. They are qualities that supplement and complement one another.

In Romans 5:1-5, Paul joins peace, joy, patience, and love to other qualities that come through the Holy Spirit. In Colossians 3:12-15 Paul mentions the interplay of kindness, meekness, patience, love, and peace with other spiritual qualities. Planted in the great "love chapter" of 1 Corinthians 13, love is irrevocably tied to patience and kindness (v. 4). Contrasting immature passions, 2 Timothy 2:22 links faith, love, and peace with righteousness. The passion of the world is contrasted with "the divine nature" in 2 Peter 1:3-8 which combines the qualities of faith, self-control, and love with other Christian virtues. Paul considers these qualities of the Spirit as essential to the unity of the body in Ephesians 4:1-3 where he speaks particularly of meekness, patience, love, and peace.

This recurring grouping of the spiritual qualities reinforces the fact that they stand together. They are qualities of the Holy Spirit and, as such, belong together to make a whole. Their combined presence in a person's life is a sign of the Holy Spirit's presence. Their absence from the life of one who professes Jesus Christ as Savior is a sign of resistance to the Holy Spirit of God, and may mean that the person has never truly trusted the Lord!

Though spiritual growth is what God expects and desires for His children, it is not inevitable. Fruit is the sign of spiritual maturity. Just as a young fruit tree will not bear fruit for a number of years, a young Christian may require some time to begin showing the effect of the transforming presence of the Holy Spirit of Christ. But that effect must begin to show, or something is dreadfully wrong! Bearing fruit is not an option chosen only by a few religious fanatics. The failure of fruit comes from a failure in one's relationship with Christ.

Jesus told a parable about a fig tree that produced no fruit:

"A man had a fig tree planted in his vineyard; and he came seeking fruit on it and found none. And he said to the vinedresser, 'Lo, these three years I have come seeking fruit on this fig tree, and I find none. Cut it down; why should it use up the ground?' And he answered him, 'Let it alone, sir, this year also, till I dig about it and put on manure. And if it bears fruit next year, well and good; but if not, you can cut it down' " (Luke 13:6-9).

When I was a boy, we had a huge fig tree beside our back porch. Its trunk was big and strong. Its foliage provided a dense canopy that shaded the porch. Best of all, its branches were covered with figs. In time, however, the branches of taller trees spread over it and cut off the light from the sun. The foliage became less dense with each passing year. The limbs became weak and broke off. Within a few years, the tree stopped bearing fruit. It became a stunted shrub, and then it died. Just like our old fig tree, Christians derive their strength and life-giving power to produce fruit from an external Source. Without the constant giving of that Source, the plant and the Christian cannot bear fruit.

Christians cannot produce a Christlike life out of their own resources any more than a fig tree can produce figs without fertile soil. The Holy Spirit is the power in a Christian's life that produces the fruit of godliness. Without that source of energy and life, Christians struggle in frustration to do what they cannot do. Yet, no Christian lacks for any of the strength and power needed to grow spiritually because the Holy Spirit has come to every believer. Then why do some grow, producing the fruit of a Christian life while others seem to atrophy?

## The Christian's Role

While the work of sanctification is the work of the Holy Spirit, Christians are not totally passive objects in the process. We have a part to play in sanctification just as we do in regeneration. God does not treat His children like objects, rather He seeks their willing cooperation. These matters weighed greatly on the mind of Christ during His last time together with His closest disciples. After supper He said to them:

> "I am the true vine, and my Father is the vinedresser. Every branch of mine that bears no fruit, he takes away, and every branch that does bear fruit he prunes, that it may bear more fruit. You are already clean by the word which I have spoken to you. Abide in me, and I in you. As the branch cannot bear fruit by itself, unless it abides in the vine, neither can you, unless you abide in me. I am the vine, you are the branches. He who abides in me, and I in him, he it is that bears much fruit, for apart from me you can do nothing. If a man does not abide in me, he is cast forth as a branch and withers; and the branches are gathered, thrown into the fire and burned. If you abide in me, and my words abide in you, ask whatever you will, and it shall be done for you. By this my Father is glorified that you bear much fruit, and so prove to be my disciples. As the Father has loved me, so have I loved you; abide in my love. If you keep my commandments, you will abide in my love, just as I have kept my Father's commandments and abide in his love. These things I have spoken to you, that my joy may be in you, and that your joy may be full" (John 15:1-11).

In this statement on the nature of Christian growth and maturity, Jesus made two dramatic points. First, Christians have no life of their own apart from Christ. This abiding in Christ involves the positive dimension of feeding and nurture. Second, bearing fruit involves a negative dimension of pruning. Within the context of these two ingredients Christian growth takes place. The absence of either of these will make growth impossible.

I love to eat fresh garden fruits and vegetables in the summertime. Allowed to ripen in the sun, they have an indescribable texture and flavor. They are so unlike the pitiful things we buy in the grocery store in January. While the store may call that spongy, hard, tasteless thing a tomato, it does not have the quality it would have had if it had remained on the vine to ripen in the sun. When the Spirit first begins to produce fruit in a Christian, it does not appear in its perfected form. Instead, spiritual growth comes through a ripening process. Too often, Christians remain content with the first appearance of spiritual fruit in their lives. Apart from close contact with Christ, the process stops like the tomatoes picked before they are ripe. By abiding in Christ, a Christian's life matures like ripening fruit.

# 2 ||| Abiding and Pruning

Christians draw their life from Christ the same way a branch draws its life from the main stem of the grapevine. Jesus made the simple comparison that a person who is not united to Him is like a branch that has been cut off the vine. The branch quickly withers. It has no life of its own, but only lives in relationship to the vine.

## Abiding

The purpose of the branch is to serve as a vehicle through which the vine expresses itself. The branch bears the fruit which the vine produces. Grapes do not appear on the trunk of the vine. The branches serve the vine by bearing the grapes. God has chosen to express His love and purposes in the world through people. Nonetheless, the fruit of a Christian's life comes from Him and comes only as a result of one's relationship to Him. Because of this relationship, Jesus said that God is glorified when Christians bear much fruit (John 15:8).

In this statement on abiding, Jesus also answered the great question of human existence: Why am I here? Human meaning finds its fulfillment in relationship to God. Because they were created to bear the fruit which God wants shown in the world, people feel cut off, lost, and isolated when they are not fulfilling their purpose. They may have no idea what their purpose is, and if told, they may not like or believe what they hear, but people everywhere know what it means to search for purpose and meaning. When cut off from God, however, people cannot fulfill the purpose for which they were created (Eph. 2:10). They cannot bear God's fruit unless they are as related and dependent upon God as a branch is to the vine.

A branch separated from its vine not only will fail to bear fruit on its own, but it will die. Jesus said that the presence of fruit, either good or bad, was an outward and visible sign of whether someone had a vital relationship with God. The presence of fruit characteristic of the Father proves that a person belongs to the Lord (John 15:8). The opposite is also true.

In a sobering comment, Jesus insisted that a person's relationship to God, whether positive or negative, would have some visible sign:

> "You will know them by their fruits. Are grapes gathered from thorns, or figs from thistles? So, every sound tree bears good fruit, but the bad tree bears evil fruit. A sound tree cannot bear evil fruit, nor can a bad tree bear good fruit. Every tree that does not bear good fruit is cut down and thrown into the fire. Thus you will know them by their fruits" (Matt. 7:16-20).

Whereas good deeds may be imitated, the spiritual qualities which indicate the essence of a person cannot be. Where good fruit issues forth, good deeds will always be present. Where bad fruit festers, however, no deed can be good because of the underlying spiritual corruption which has motivated it.

Paul said that Christians are like wild olive branches that have been grafted on to a domestic tree, so the wild branches are able then to benefit from the richness of the good tree (Rom. 11:17). The quality of the fruit depends upon its root source. A wild branch may bear fruit of a sort just as a rebellious person may do what the world judges to be good. Monuments and testimonials, awards and honors, may all be conferred by a grateful world on some noble benefactor who at heart is corrupt. The quality of persons' lives, however, does not depend on the deeds they do but on the root that generates their deeds.

Paul understood that a bad tree—or person—can perform good deeds and still be a bad tree. He confessed, "If I give away all I have, and if I deliver my body to be burned, but have not love, I gain nothing" (1 Cor. 13:3). Deeds of piety are only vain striving unless accompanied by a heart transformed by God. Jesus warned the religious community to beware the manner in which they practiced their piety. Religious devotion and good deeds can have their motivation in a variety of sources (Matt. 6:1-18). For an act of benevolence to be completely void of selfish motives, guilt, or other causes, it must be an act of love created by the abiding relationship with Christ. The absence of works of piety indicates an absence of genuine fruit (Jas. 2:14 *ff*).

By abiding in Christ, a person opens the channels by which God feeds a soul and produces spiritual fruit. Spiritual nourishment occurs in a reciprocal process of obedience to the Lord and prayer. In keeping the commandments of Christ, Christians abide in Christ's love (John 15:10) and see their prayers answered (John 14:7,16).

## Obedience

Obedience is not a condition for earning the love and hearing of God, nor is it a condition for being nourished spiritually by God. Instead, *obedience* is the means God uses to bestow love and blessing. Keeping His commandments is the way Christians are nourished.

Abiding in Christ involves the reciprocal situation of Christ's words abiding in the believer as the believer abides in Christ. More is involved than an intellectual awareness of Christ's teachings or a memorization of His sayings. Abiding involves life itself. If the life of the vine does not enter the branches, they die. Christ's words become the basis for living when they abide in the believer.

When the word of Christ abides in a believer, it becomes an integral part of life. Jesus compared it to the foundation of a house; without the foundation, the house cannot stand against the natural forces of wind, rain, and flood (Matt. 7:24-27). The house depends upon the foundation for support in time of need. For the word of Christ to be foundational in a believer's life, the believer must do what Christ has said. Christ did not deliver an arbitrary set of commandments to oppress His disciples; instead, His words were a gift of help and deliverance to preserve the believer.

To obey the words of Christ, however, one must have a firm faith in the One who spoke those words. Doing what Jesus says forms the outward and visible sign that a person actually believes Jesus is the King of kings and Lord of lords. Doing what Jesus says is the tangible demonstration that a believer loves the Lord (John 14:15,23-24). Obedience, then, becomes a conduit for receiving the love of Christ: "If you keep my commandments, you will abide in my love, just as I have kept my Father's commandments and abide in his love" (John 15:10).

## Prayer

Obedience is the context in which God's Spirit nourishes the Christian. Obedience is also the context in which prayer has nurturing power. Abiding in Christ involves a closeness that only prayer can bring. The power of prayer comes from the vine/branch relationship. The branch exists to express the purpose of the vine. The Christian exists to express the purpose of Christ. When a Christian prays, truly desiring the will of God, that prayer has incredible power.

Through His prayers, Jesus abode in the Father and the Father in Him. When the eternal Christ emptied Himself of His glory by coming into the world (John 17:5; Phil. 2:6-7), His oneness with the Father was maintained by Their Holy Spirit and Their constant conversation. Jesus had but one thing in mind in His conversation with the Father—that the Father should be glorified and His purpose accomplished. The prayers of a Christian in whom the fruit of Christ's Spirit appears brings glory to God. God empowers such a person with answered prayer.

Unfortunately, many Christians pray like anorexics eat! Some anorexics eat nothing at all, to speak of, and starve themselves. Christians deny themselves the nurture and power necessary to produce the fruit of Christ's character when they neglect prayer, the greatest privilege a Christian enjoys. A Christian who neglects the privilege of prayer is as self-destructive as a person who refuses to eat. By His atoning death, Christ opened the access to God and became our high priest making constant intercession for us. On this account the New Testament urges us to "draw near" (Heb. 10:19-22).

People with bulimia have a different attitude toward food. Rather than neglecting it, they gorge themselves on it. Then, immediately upon finishing the meal, they purge themselves of all that they have eaten. Food may be used for one's own purpose rather than the purpose for which God intended it. The same can be said of prayer. Praying is a fruitless exercise if it is only designed to gratify the passions and desires of the one who prays. While one form of spiritual immaturity does not believe in the power of prayer at all, another form of spiritual immaturity only regards prayer as a way of getting what one wants. Either of these attitudes toward prayer will fail to produce fruit.

Unless a person has a balanced view of the power of prayer, he or she really should not bother to read any more of this book. If prayer does not make a difference, then certainly nothing else makes any difference either. Of course, some folks argue that prayer awakens in them a concern and commitment to get involved in a situation enough to make a difference. Others see the power of prayer in the way it helps them get in touch with themselves so that they can cope with life situations. Still others regard prayer as a way of touching base with God who, though He cannot interfere with the course of nature and human events, certainly wishes us all the best. These ideas of prayer are not what I mean by the power of prayer.

By the power of prayer, I mean those times when a situation is humanly hopeless, but God changes everything as a result of a specific request. The power of prayer is seen in the intervention by God in the natural course of events and nature. The scarcity of the manifestation of the power of prayer is in direct inverse proportion to the number of Christians who do not abide in Christ as our Lord desired. Yet, the power of prayer also occurs when we find peace with God even though our requests may go unanswered. The power of prayer rests ultimately in the awesome experience of free and open communication with God.

Prayer is not a magician's formula for obtaining power over the universe. A person who prays must surrender to the Power of the universe. The power of prayer may mean the miracle of Lazarus rising from the dead (John 11:41-44), but it may also mean dying a horrible death to accomplish God's purpose (Luke 22:42). Either way, it makes little difference for one who abides in Christ. Prayers are always for the glory of God. Through such prayers, Christ abides in the believer just as the Father abides in the Son.

## Pruning

Jesus said that "every branch that does bear fruit he prunes, that it may bear more fruit" (John 15:2). For most of my early life I could not understand why people pruned their fruit trees. In South Carolina where I grew up, we produced an enormous amount of peaches. My mother used to take us to Watson's peach orchard to pick peaches. The trees were thick with peaches and luxuriant foliage, but each year the limbs were cut back to the trunk of the tree. I thought it was a waste. Why not let those limbs grow and grow and grow?

When I moved to Kentucky, our neighbors had a peach tree. They thought it was a shame to prune back the limbs every year, so they let the tree grow and take its own course. Instead of the strong, sturdy trunk of the trees back home, its trunk is thin and willowy. Instead of the thick, lush foliage, its foliage is sparse and scraggly. Worst of all, instead of the softball-size peaches that covered the Watson's trees, its fruit is small and hard like golf balls and only speckles the tree here and there.

Pruning does not detract from a fruit tree's beauty; it enhances it. Pruning is not a punishment for a Christian; it is a reward. God is the vinedresser who prunes the life of everyone who abides in Christ and bears the fruit of Christ. Spiritual pruning enhances spiritual growth by removing whatever inhibits spiritual growth.

Through much of life we are told that things do not hurt. When our little cocker spaniel had its tail clipped, I was told it would not hurt. Other dogs have their ears clipped, and we are told it does not hurt. Show horses have their tails broken to look the part, but for some reason it is not supposed to hurt. Lies, lies, lies! Of course it hurts. All serious pruning hurts. The amputation of a leg consumed by gangrene hurts, but it saves a life.

For some reason, however, Christians seem surprised that spiritual pruning may be painful. Freedom from pain and suffering is a promise of a Christian's future glorification, but pain and suffering are a part of present sanctification. The pain of spiritual pruning is a result of our reluctance to give up whatever inhibits our growth. Christians do not like to be pruned any more than children like to receive shots. It hurts. Whenever the Lord prunes us, we lose a part of ourselves. Habits, attitudes, and thoughts are as much a part of us as our faces, arms, and legs. To have part of our spiritual being pruned is to lose part of who we are. Pruning changes who we are.

Without the pruning, we remain all foliage and no fruit. Since Adam and Eve, however, people have liked having plenty of foliage in their lives to hide behind. Spiritual foliage is an outward show. It covers up who we are sometimes. It creates a costume for being something other than what God wants us to be. Unless a Christian is careful, the show of foliage can become a substitute for the substance of fruit.

For some Christians, the foliage that requires pruning is "a form of godliness." In the Sermon on the Mount, Jesus went into great detail to show the defect of false piety. The outward act of piety or the habitual practice of piety can be nothing but show if the spirit that motivates the piety is false. Jesus warned, "Beware of practicing your piety before men in order to be seen by them; for then you will have no reward from your Father who is in heaven" (Matt. 6:1). In His discourse on piety and faith found in Matthew 6 and 7, Jesus hacked away at the form of religion to reach the substance of faith. Unfortunately, many Christians happily prefer to settle for the form.

The sobering danger of settling for the form of religion without the substance of faith was demonstrated by Jesus in perhaps His most disturbing act. Upon finding nothing but leaves on a fig tree when He was hungry, Jesus cursed the tree, and it died (Matt. 21:18-22). Today, most people ask why He did it. Scholarship is perplexed for want of an explanation since one would not normally have expected to find figs during the Passover. The disciples, on the other hand, asked a more elemental question: How did You do it? In His answer, Jesus immediately focused on the primacy of faith and prayer in daily life. The cursing of the fig tree was a living parable of the uselessness of form (leaves) without the substance of faith (fruit).

Something else beside foliage is pruned away to produce fruit. If the fruit tree has dead limbs, these limbs become a way for rot, disease, and insects to enter the tree and kill it. Unless the deadness is cut out, it will spread like a cancer until the whole tree is consumed. Left unchecked, sin extends its control over every part of a Christian's life. Sin prevents fruitfulness. Toleration of sin invites the introduction of other forms of sin. Sin is the enemy of the Spirit of God and prevents Christians from being like Christ. In Galatians, Paul says: "The desires of the flesh are against the Spirit, and the desires of the Spirit are against the flesh; for these are opposed to each other, to prevent you from doing what you would" (5:17). Part of the work of the Holy Spirit in sanctification is pruning out the sin in a Christian's life.

The greatest problem in dealing with sin rests in the human reluctance to recognize and confess its presence. We can deal with sin in theory, as long as it remains vague and nebulous. Few Christians have difficulty praying, "Forgive us of all our many sins." Somehow we even feel holier for admitting we are just like everyone else, and we all have many sins. It becomes more difficult, however, to confess what those many sins happen to be.

It is easier to recognize "all my sins" than to face the fact that I am a jealous person. It is easier to confess "all my sins" than to confess self-pity. It is easier to acknowledge "all my sins" in theory than to deal with a single one specifically. As long as sin is nameless and face-less, we can continue to ignore it. Jesus said that when the Holy Spirit came He would convince the world of sin (John 16:8). Jesus knew that people do not want to face the fact of sin, even if it means their own self-destruction. Simply put, we do not want our sins exposed: "For every one who does evil hates the light, and does not come to the light, lest his deeds should be exposed" (John 3:20). If we willingly gave up our sins, the pruning would not be as painful.

Conviction of sin constitutes only one dimension of spiritual prun-ing. My grandfather had a next-door neighbor who had a huge apple tree, but some of its limbs were dead. My grandfather pointed these out to the man many times, but the man did nothing about it. Because he did nothing, disease set in, and the fruit became gnarled and worth-less. Conviction of sin does not automatically result in pruning. Knowledge of sin does not force repentance. My grandfather's neigh-bor was willing to live with the facts. Cutting out the dead limbs was too much trouble. For many Christians, growing to spiritual maturity is too much trouble and conflicts with their selfish desires.

When Christians become stubborn and refuse to cooperate with the Holy Spirit, God deals more sternly with them. The metaphor of the natural process of growth and fruit bearing is left behind. God then deals with us as defiant children who have their own ideas about what they want to be. All of the imagery of fruit in the Bible is just a poetic way of saying that an apple tree is like an apple tree, and a Christian is like Christ. In talking about fruit, we should never lose sight of the fact that Christians are supposed to be spiritual chips off the old block; like Father, like Son.

Hebrews reminds us that God will go to great lengths to accomplish the pruning, with or without our cooperation. The pruning that re-sults may be far more painful than should be necessary:

> "My son, do not regard lightly the discipline of the Lord,
> nor lose courage when you are punished by him.
> For the Lord disciplines him whom he loves,
> and chastises every son whom he receives."

It is for discipline that you have to endure. God is treating you as sons; for what son is there whom his father does not discipline? If you are left without discipline, in which all have participated, then you are illegitimate children and not sons. Besides this, we have had earthly fathers to discipline us and we respected them. Shall we not much more be subject to the Father of spirits and live? For they disciplined us for a short time at their pleasure, but he disciplines us for our good, that we may share his holiness. For the moment all discipline seems painful rather than pleasant; later it yields the peaceful fruit of righteousness to those who have been trained by it (Heb. 12:5-11).

The goal of God's discipline is to bring His children into conformity with His holiness which manifests itself as the "peaceful fruit of righteousness."

Even with the discipline of the Lord, however, some Christians have the will to resist pruning. Paul warned the Corinthians that Christians hopelessly bound to a sin that they refuse to give up will be removed from the world for their ultimate spiritual safety (1 Cor. 5:5). He flatly stated that this condition of unrepented sin had brought about both sickness and death in the Corinthian church (1 Cor. 11:30).

The positive teaching of the New Testament in light of the prospect of discipline is for the Christian not only to cooperate with, but to long for, this miraculous work of God. We are encouraged to examine ourselves in a regular, disciplined fashion for glimpses of those matters in our hearts which are contrary to the Spirit of Christ (1 Cor. 11:27-32; 2 Cor. 13:5). Rather than being self-righteous in comparison to the failings of other Christians, we are encouraged to use their failings as warnings to ourselves and as guides for self-examination (Gal. 6:1).

The most important theme for sanctification which the New Testament sounds, however, appears immediately before the warning about discipline in Hebrews. It is presented as the positive alternative to what comes afterward. Looking to Christ exposes to our hearts what needs to be laid aside:

> Let us also lay aside every weight, and sin which clings so closely, and let us run with perseverance the race that is set before us, looking to Jesus the pioneer and perfecter of our faith, who for the joy that was set before him endured the cross, despising the shame, and is seated at the right hand of the throne of God.
>
> Consider him who endured from sinners such hostility against himself, so that you may not grow weary or fainthearted (12:1-3).

Christians do not overcome sin when they think about the sin. As often as not, they only become more attracted to the sin! Only by focusing on Jesus does the sin begin to lose its hold. By actively striving in a positive way to be Christlike, what is not Christlike can be pruned. It falls away like scales because the passions and desires of the flesh have been supplanted by the passions and desires of the Spirit.

Throughout the New Testament, we find the positive appeal for Christians to focus on Christ and be like God. Rather than being caught up in the transient glory of the world, which panders to the passions and desires of the human heart, the New Testament urges Christians to glimpse the eternal glory of God and the imperishable nature of godly affections. By his continual return to the greater reality of spirit, Paul could face impossible hardships and sacrifice luxury and advantage while declaring, "I consider that the sufferings of this present time are not worth comparing with the glory that is to be revealed to us" (Rom. 8:18). When we open our lives to the Spirit of Christ alive in us, He begins to produce the fruit of His presence in our lives.

# 3 ||| Love

When I was at Oxford, I had a conversation with a man who struggled with his spiritual life. He had searched for God for a number of years, wondering if indeed there was a God. We had a long conversation one evening in the Junior Commons Room of Regent's Park College, and in the course of that conversation the man kept talking about Jesus and the whole concept of love that Christianity is supposed to embody. He was upset by the idea that Jesus commanded His disciples to love.

Jesus did give His disciples the command to love (John 13:34), but even more so, to love their enemies (Matt. 5:44). He told us to love those who hate us and to pray for those who persecute us. This command upset my friend, because he said he could not just turn love on and off like a switch. He felt people could not control their emotions to that extent. He said that people could not will to feel a certain way about someone else.

He carried the conversation further and began to wonder if love is nothing more than a code of morality. He could deal with love as a moral code if that is what Christianity means by love, but he wanted to know if that is what Jesus meant.

## The Command to Love

Jesus did command His disciples to love. In fact, the night He was taken, the night they gathered in the upper room, He said, "This I command you, to love one another" (John 15:17). "I command you, to love." For Jesus, love is something that can be commanded, and we are expected to obey. As we look at what Jesus and the New Testament say about love, we discover that love is not simply an emotion. We rarely have the opportunity to show "Christian" love to people close to us. People with whom we are deeply involved, like our parents, siblings, children, and close friends, rarely become the recipients of our Christian love. Those deep, intimate relationships have too much giving and receiving in return.

## More Than Reciprocity

Jesus said that this kind of love marked by giving and receiving is not unusual. It is not restricted to Christians, and people all over the world, both good and bad, experience this kind of love. This kind of love marks the giving and receiving in a marriage or in a friendship. Jesus said that even the heathen have warm feelings for those that are close to them (Luke 6:32-33). This principle of reciprocity which we see in intimate relationships is not the sort of love that can be commanded. In a sense, it is an investment. We give knowing that we are going to receive something in return.

This experience of love is not necessarily bad. Knowing that someone else loves us and shares in this constant giving and receiving is one of the beautiful experiences that makes life worthwhile. But true love of the type Jesus talked about, this perfect love that He commands us to have, emerges in deep personal relationships only when all the benefits are gone. It can emerge when the warm feelings suddenly or gradually subside. It can emerge when the old romantic stirrings of marriage have faded. It can emerge when we find that our parents are too old and feeble to do anything for us anymore, and life becomes a matter of constantly doing for them. It can emerge when old relationships become a constant demand and drain on us. It can emerge when friends betray us, let us down, or neglect us. In these sorts of crisis moments, suddenly we have the opportunity for love as Jesus speaks of it. It is not the emotion that we feel at such times but the shear exercise of the will that "I will love."

## More Than Passionate Desire

Holy love is not characterized by what Paul mentions in Galatians as passion or desire for something. Even in marriage, love seeks or desires something. In marriage there is a seeking of the other person. Marriage contains a certain selfishness that might be expressed, "I want that person to be with me, and me alone." The sort of love that brings people together in marriage contains an element of self-seeking, but Paul mentions in 1 Corinthians 13 that "love does not insist on its own way." It is not self-interested or out for its own gratification.

In Charles Dickens's novel, *A Tale of Two Cities*, the climax came when a family was in deep trouble. The husband was about to be executed during the Reign of Terror in Paris, and the man who loved the hero's wife had the strange gift of being virtually identical in appearance to the condemned man. Had the hero died, perhaps this character would have had the opportunity to court the dead man's wife. Instead, he substituted himself for the hero, through trickery, thus becoming the hero himself. He went to the guillotine and died in place of the other with the words, "Tis a far better thing I do than I have ever done before." In this bit of fiction one sees the sort of love that is not self-interested but is self-giving, knowing that nothing will ever come back in return.

## More Than Emotion

Holy love is not an emotion that can be snuffed out. The apostle Paul said that love never ends (1 Cor. 13:8). Marriage relationships can end, friendships can end, and brothers and sisters can despise one another, but true love as Christ spoke of it never ends. When the crisis comes that kills emotions and destroys feelings, love bears all things (1 Cor. 13:7). Love believes all things, love hopes all things, and love endures all things. It is not an emotion that comes and goes, rather it is an attitude and an action that can be willed and commanded: "I will stick it out! I will help those persons no matter how stubborn and obnoxious they are!"

It is interesting to note that when Jesus was asked to explain what loving one's neighbor meant, He gave the example of a Samaritan. He told of a Samaritan helping a stranger, someone with whom that Samaritan's only emotional and personal involvement was mutual racial bigotry. The Samaritan responded from the deep-seated attitude that if someone needed his help, he was going to help the person. Love is more than a feeling. It is an attitude for living that can be willed.

## The Act of Love

Another thing Jesus said about this kind of love is that it is given without hope of reward. Often the love that we give in such a case is in spite of the behavior of the person we are loving. God and how He acts is what love really is. So often we take love as we experience it on earth, see that love is mentioned in the Bible, and conclude that our experiences equal spiritual love. But Jesus took a different approach to defining love. Look first at what God does and how He does it, then you begin to get an idea of what love means. Jesus said that God sends the rain on the just and the unjust alike (Matt. 5:45). God loves both categories of people. He lets the sun come up on the fields of the wicked just as He lets the sun come up on the fields of the righteous. Love is doing things for people who do not appreciate it.

## Love as Charity

Despite all the advances in modern translations of the Bible, the *King James Version* of 1611 probably translates the idea of love in 1 Corinthians 13 better than any other. When I first went to seminary, I learned that the Greek word the *King James Version* translates *charity* is translated in most other places in the New Testament as *love*. The modern translators have tended to discard the word *charity* and replace it with *love*. By losing the idea of charity in love, we have also lost the sense behind the command of Jesus to love. Regaining the understanding of charity in our idea of love is essential to our being able to *do* love. The word *love* has the idea of emotion and feeling about it, but *charity* is something people do.

The Latin word found in the Vulgate, from which the translators in 1611 derived the word *charity*, has the concept of costliness in its root meaning. This kind of love—charity—is costly. It is expensive to express. It costs a person something to show it. Even the tax collectors loved people who loved them back. Jesus asked His audience point blank if they saluted just their brothers, just their friends, just those that were close to them, or just those who could return the favor. If they loved only these people, what were they doing differently from everyone else? Didn't even the Gentiles do the same (Matt. 5:46-47)? Love, on the other hand, costs us something because we do not get anything back when we love.

Love also governs our attitudes toward people. Abraham Lincoln used *charity* this way in his second inaugural address: "With malice toward none; with charity for all." Lincoln was speaking of his enemies, the ones the Union Army was fighting and killing on the battlefields—those vociferous Southerners. Charity—love—should mark our attitude toward our enemies, Jesus said, especially those who hate us or persecute us. Love characterizes the Christian's attitude because God is our example of what love is.

## Love as Attitude

Jesus said, "You, therefore, must be perfect, as your heavenly father is perfect" (Matt. 5:48). Because Christians are the children of God, their lives must be like His life. Since the Spirit of God dwells in all Christians, their lives must be like His life. Yet God loves those who sin against Him. He sends the sun and the rain for those who sin against Him, but most remarkably, "God commendeth his love toward us, in that, while we were yet sinners, Christ died for us" (Rom. 5:8, KJV). Love characterizes God and the way God deals with the world, His enemies, and all people. The Bible says that while we were still enemies, we were reconciled to God through the death of His Son. Love is the attitude of God. It is costly, for it cost Him His Son, but it is a free gift motivated by caring concern.

In the Old Testament, the loving that characterizes God is called "steadfast love." In Hebrew it is the same word that is translated "mercy." *Mercy* is God's attitude toward those who need mercy. I had a friend in college who managed to "squeeze" four years of study into eight. In only two more years, he would have graduated if he had kept going. But he had a wonderful time in college until the end of each semester rolled around. Then he would go to visit each of his professors and plead with them, "Don't give me justice, give me mercy." *Love* is not giving people what they deserve or desire; *love* is giving people what they need.

## The Proof of Discipleship

Jesus told us another thing about love; it proves we are His disciples. Love enables people to tell whether or not we are Christians. It is the only sign we find in Scriptures that is universally applied to all Christians. How are we treating one another? Jesus spoke of this identifying mark of Christianity the night He was taken: "A new commandment I give to you, that you love one one another; even as I have loved you, that you also love one another. By this all men will know that you are my disciples, if you have love for one another" (John 13:34-35). John wrote that down. He thought it was important.

John was one of the Sons of Thunder, and a son of thunder was not characterized by love. On the contrary, he tended to blast off at people when he had the opportunity. John was changed radically when love became a characteristic of his life, and the whole concept electrified him. "Beloved," he said, "if God so loved us, we also ought to love one another.... If any one says 'I love God,' and hates his brother, he is a liar; for he who does not love his brother whom he has seen, cannot love God whom he has not seen. And this commandment we have from him, that he who loves God should love his brother also" (1 John 4:11, 20-21). Love is something we will. It is something we do whether we feel like it or not. It is something that can be commanded.

During World War II in Rome, a Catholic priest in the Vatican was involved in smuggling Jews out of Rome to escape the gestapo. While the gestapo busily tried to track down the priest and uncover his network, he busily sent people to safety. The priest's work could be seen as an act of love, and indeed it was, but that was not the ultimate test of this priest's love. As the war came to an end and the Allied armies were grouped around Rome, the commander of the gestapo sent an agent to infiltrate the Vatican and bring out the priest. Instead of killing the priest, however, the gestapo commander asked a favor. He wanted the priest to smuggle his wife and children out of Rome to safety. He wanted the priest to save his family. The man who was responsible for sending hundreds upon hundreds of people to concentration camps and to death wanted the priest, whom he had tried to apprehend, to have mercy on his family. The priest was outraged by the idea. This monster who had shown no compassion now wanted mercy. The priest refused to help. The German's family could suffer the consequences of his life.

"So," the German said contemptuously, "there is nothing at all to this love you Christians talk about."

When the Allied troops entered Rome, they arrested the gestapo agent and interrogated him. They wanted to know the name of the mastermind behind the underground group that had smuggled his family out of the country. The German fell dumbfounded and silent, not knowing how to explain it. For the next fifteen years that priest came once a week to visit this gestapo commander in prison. Finally, after all those years, the commander accepted the rule of Jesus Christ as his Savior, yet he did not deserve mercy.

Jesus never gave us the option of deciding who does and who does not deserve love and mercy. He came and died on the cross for the people of the world, none of whom deserve it, and He loves every creature on earth. God expects His children to have the same attitude He has. Love is not the warm feeling we have for the people close to us; it is what we do for the ones who do not deserve it.

The Bible teaches that bearing fruit involves both pruning and fertilizing. Those parts of us which are unwilling to love must be pruned before we can love as Christ commanded. The unwillingness to love may extend to other members of a church with whom personalities have clashed. It may extend to members of our family we cannot stand to be around. It may extend to people in the community we find irritating and obnoxious. It may extend to strangers who have committed the sin of being different from us. The attitude of unwillingness to love must be sacrificed to the Lord before love can blossom into fruit in the life of a Christian.

For the Spirit to enable us love, we must be fed. Fertilization needs to accompany pruning. Jesus told His disciples to gain this added strength, nourishment, and ability to love those who do not deserve it by praying for them. He gives us the unlikely instruction to pray for those who persecute us. Jesus knew the impossibility of praying for people without becoming concerned about them and involved with them. Prayer gives the power, strength, and ability for bearing the fruit of love which people cannot muster from their own resources. The command to love involves doing something divine, which is impossible without divine involvement.

# 4 ||| Joy

C. S. Lewis entitled his spiritual autobiography *Surprised by Joy*. Lewis thought of joy as the most singular experience imaginable, unlike anything else. He used words like *delight, bliss, rapture,* and *ecstasy* to describe the experience of joy. None of these, however, quite expresses what joy really means.

In the previous discussion of love, the argument was presented that love is not so much what we feel but what we do as Christians. Joy, on the other hand, is the feeling that complements that love. Lewis found our deep religious experiences to be the most meaningful of human experience and the one thing that kept drawing him on toward faith in Christ.

### Joy as Longing

Lewis discovered in his conversion that joy has a dark side as well as a light side. Joy involves longing just as it involves fulfillment. This longing amounts to more than a desire for something. Paul refers to *desire* in the Galatians passage on the fruit of the Spirit, and he says that Christians have been freed from the passion of desire, which might also be called lust. Desire can be a trivial lust, such as wanting a car or a stereo. There are all kinds of things we desire to possess, but these things are merely ornaments to life like ornaments on a Christmas tree. Ornaments do not affect the tree at all. They just hang there.

Last year we were late buying a Christmas tree, and what we finally found looked more like the parsley that garnished our Christmas turkey. We hung beautiful decorations on the tree, thinking we would hide the ridiculous tree itself. When friends dropped by, they never noticed the ornaments; they only laughed at our misshaped sprig of a tree.

## Longing as Spiritual Thirst

Longing involves more than the lusts that camouflage our lives. Longing involves our very survival. It is like thirst. Thirst can only be satisfied by having a drink. If I am thirsty, I do not want a steak. If I am thirsty, nothing I eat will satisfy my thirst. When I thirst, I must have something to drink. This sort of longing ultimately involves survival. The longer I go without having the longing met, the stronger the longing will grow. If it is never met, I will die.

Homesickness may be related to this kind of desire. Homesickness is the felt need to be in a particular place with particular people; no other house and no other group of people will satisfy that longing. Such longings can affect our health and behavior.

Nothing can satisfy longing except the one thing that is longed for. The strange thing about this longing is that it cannot be sought. It cannot be pursued the way pleasure or fun can be pursued. One may find pleasure. One may find fun. Our society gears itself to providing pleasure and fun. Unfortunately, people usually confuse joy with its imitations. They settle for pleasure and never find joy.

Things can bring pleasure, but they can never bring joy because they do not reach into our spirits. The same sort of circumstance occurs when people laugh at a joke when they are depressed or in a miserable mood. It is possible to laugh at such times, but the joke does not reach deeply enough into the spirit to make a person happy. Laughter is not happiness any more than pleasure is joy.

## Longing as Dissatisfaction

Lewis said that joy must have a stab or a pang of inconsolable longing that nothing else can satisfy. Because of this longing, joy creates a dissatisfaction with any other state of mind. Joy will not let people settle for anything less. The longing gives us the knowledge that there is something more, something better to life, even if we have never experienced it. This knowledge is the work of the Holy Spirit. Longing tells us that there is something missing from our lives. We cannot describe what that missing experience is, but we know it is there. Lewis experienced this longing until his conversion. Then he knew what that unknown experience was.

People drive themselves in a quest for this missing ingredient of life.

Some pursue it through the drug culture while others take an alternative route through fame and fortune, reputation and respectability, success and sociability. Yet, nothing can quench this thirsting of the spirit except joy.

## The Source of Joy

If joy does not come through grabbing for it, then how does it come? How can a person experience joy? In the Bible, the experience of joy comes through relationships. Things may give pleasure, but only people can give joy. Joy can only come as a gift, and it can only come from a person. People give joy as a gift. Joy cannot be acquired by forcibly taking it. It cannot be squeezed out of life. Lewis was right. Joy surprises us. It comes to us from outside, like a surprise birthday party. Though it is possible to manipulate people and drop hints or sneak around to discover if someone is giving us a party, when we do that we lose the one crucial ingredient of a surprise party—it is no longer a surprise.

Joy is like that. The more we want that feeling of joy and the more we try to get it, the more it eludes us. Joy has to be given to us. In Greek, the word for *joy* and the word for *grace* come from the same root word. Joy is *chara*, and grace is *charis*. *Grace* is a free gift; it is completely unearned or unmerited. *Joy* is also something that comes to us.

### Joy as Relationship

Joy comes in the presence or in the thought of the one who is loved. King David understood this. David was the great king of Israel. He was the model of what a king should be, but if we look at his career, we find that from time to time he was overtaken by sin. At one particular point in David's life, he became involved in an affair with a married woman. As usually happens in those situations, one disaster led to another. In order to cover up the affair, David arranged to have the husband neatly put away in the heat of battle. And so, Uriah the Hittite fell in death. David thought his sin was neatly covered up. It was hidden from everyone except God. David found that his relationship with God had crumbled and shattered. He prayed this prayer:

Cast me not away from thy presence,
and take not thy holy Spirit from me.
Restore unto me the joy of thy salvation (Ps. 51:11-12).

Despite David's imperfections, the Bible tells us he was a man after God's own heart. Even though he had been distracted by things, side-tracked by seeking pleasure, and wrapped up in physical experiences, there was something for which he longed more than passing pleasure. He longed for the presence of God. He was a man after God's heart. When he compared his empire, his harem, his riches, and his power to being in the presence of God, nothing else mattered. Nothing compared with the presence of God, and he pleaded, "Cast me not away from thy presence." Away from God's presence, David did not have joy anymore. Life without joy is no life at all.

## Joy as By-Product

All his early life, C. S. Lewis sought that experience which he called joy. He failed to create it. He failed to make it come to him. Then, when Lewis found his Lord—trusted Christ Jesus as the one who brought him salvation—he was suddenly surprised by joy. He had not planned it. He had not expected it. It just reached out and hugged him and held him. Joy is the experience a person has in being close to God. It is a common experience of conversion.

Charles Finney, the great evangelist of the first half of the nineteenth century gave this account of his conversion:

> Without any expectation of it, without ever having the thought in my mind that there was any such thing for me, without any recollection that I had heard the thing mentioned by any person in the world, the Holy Spirit descended upon me in a manner that seemed to go through my body and soul. I could feel the impression like a wave of electricity going through and through. Indeed, it seemed to come in waves and waves of liquid love because I could not express it in any other way. It seemed like the very breath of God. I can recollect distinctly that it seemed to fan me like immense wings. No words can express the wonderful love that was shed abroad in my heart. I wept aloud with joy.[1]

Joy may be charged with emotion, like Finney's conversion, or it may be quiet and penetrating like Lewis's conversion, which he described this way.

I know very well when, but hardly how the final step was taken. I was driven to Whipsnade one sunny morning. When we set out, I did not believe that Jesus Christ is the Son of God. And when we reached the zoo I did. Yet, I had not exactly spent the journey in thought, nor in great emotion. Emotional is perhaps the last word we can apply to some of the most important events. It was more like when a man after long sleep still lying motionless in bed becomes aware that he is now awake.[2]

Joy comes in the morning and surprises us. It touches us and supplies that missing ingredient in life that satisfies the longing of our spirits.

Joy does not come in what God does for us. It does not come in the wonders and the miracles God might perform. Demonstrations of His power may create wonder and amazement, but they do not create joy. Demonstrations of His power may create fear or thanksgiving, but they do not create joy. Joy comes by God's presence. Joy is the experience we have in being close to such a wonderful person who cares about us. This experience comes in friendships: the joy of having someone special who cares about us. Joy comes when we have that sort of relationship with God. If God never did anything at all, it would be joyous just to be in His presence.

## Joy as the Well-Being of Others

Jesus told several parables about people who were full of joy. Remember the shepherd who had gone in search of one lamb that was lost? He went out into the danger of the hillside where not only lambs, but also shepherds, fall prey to lions and wolves. Not only lambs but also shepherds fall over cliffs in the dark. In spite of the danger, the shepherd went out into the darkness to retrieve that frail creature in such desperate need. When he found it, he went back to town to gather together his friends to rejoice with him. He could not contain his joy. He had to share it with other people to experience the full joy.

Jesus also told of a woman who lost a coin. Her distress did not come from a simple loss of wealth. In those days when a woman was married, she received some coins that were her dowry. They had been in the family for years, passed from mother to daughter. They symbolized a very special relationship with someone and with the family that had nurtured her. The coin represented relationships that were a part of who she was. The coin was such a precious part of her that she stopped at nothing to find it. She turned the house upside down, and when she found it, she gathered the neighbors together to rejoice with her. She could not contain the joy. It had to be shared.

Finally, Jesus mentioned a father whose son had rejected him, his life-style, his teaching, and had gone off into the world. When the father regained his son, he had to share his joy with someone, and he went out to find the older brother to see if he would rejoice and share the joy. Jesus said, "There is joy before the angels of God over one sinner who repents" (Luke 15:10). The Lord knows our frailty and our deep need. The Lord knows how desperate human life is. The Lord entered into this world not just to know it intellectually, through the infinite wisdom of God, but actually to experience what it is like to be rejected by family and friends; He was a person who could be insulted, injured, harmed, and even murdered. God knows our every weakness and frailty, and He knows our need. Therefore, when our well-being comes about, God is filled with joy. It is the same with us.

Oddly enough, joy often follows sadness or tragedy. When those we love and care about are in deep need and suddenly begin to experience well-being, we experience joy with them because we love them. The relationship is the context of joy. However, joy is not constant in life. Jesus did not imply that it was. In fact He warned His disciples that sorrow would overtake them. He said, "So you have sorrow now, but I will see you again and your hearts will rejoice, and no one will take your joy from you" (John 16:22). When sorrow comes, it is hard to experience joy. When we love someone who is going through pain, the joy diminishes. The joy is gone because we are experiencing the pain with the person. Jesus promises us that the sorrow will pass away because something lies beyond the sorrow.

## Joy as the Bridge Beyond Sadness

The joy of Christ lay beyond the suffering of the cross. We are told in Hebrews about Christ "who for the joy that was set before him endured the cross, despising the shame, and is seated at the right hand of the throne of God" (12:2). Jesus' joy lay on the other side of sorrow. His joy did not consist in being the King of kings and Lord of lords. His joy did not consist in having the crown and the power and the glory. The joy of the Lord was to be in the presence of His Father again, to be at the hand of His Father. That relationship provided His source of joy. Nothing else could bring it. We can endure sorrow and sadness better when we know what lies ahead. Jesus Christ has given us the concrete hope of what lies just beyond the sorrow. He has given us promises about the future. Paul said, "I know whom I have believed" (2 Tim. 1:12). Paul knew that Christ was able to keep that which Paul had committed unto Him. The basis for joy is our relationship with Jesus Christ.

## The Loss of Joy

While sorrow may blur the vision of joy, the saddest loss of joy comes by choice. People do not decide they will not have joy, but they do decide to live in a way that banishes joy. Before describing how Christ endured the cross for the joy beyond, Hebrews gives a warning: "Let us also lay aside every weight, and sin which clings so closely, and let us run with perseverance the race that is set before us, looking to Jesus" (Heb. 12:1-2).

When the joy has left a relationship, any relationship, a wall has grown up that must be torn down. It may happen because of distraction or apathy, but whenever joy seems to have faded, sin seems to be involved. Sin denies Christians the joy of their relationship with Jesus Christ. Jesus told us that He prunes every branch that bears fruit, so it may bear more. Sin must be pruned, otherwise, joy will not bloom.

Because joy comes in nearness to God, anything that inhibits closeness with God must be pruned. Worship often hinders rather than encourages a sense of joy. When we become too familiar with worship, we lose a sense of the presence of Christ. As worship becomes a routine dominated by complacency, the longing for nearness with God can be replaced by a smug satisfaction that some debt has been discharged. Doing "holy things" can become a substitute for longing after God that will eventually kill the longing.

Instead of an attitude of complacency in worship, Christians need to worship in the belief of Christ's promise that He has a special presence in worship, wherever two or three are gathered in His name. Surely, Christ is present when Christians are alone, but He promised a special visitation for Christians who gather in His name for worship. Such gathering presupposes a longing after Christ that He wants to satisfy. Jesus Christ wants to fill His disciples with joy.

King David understood well that sin had come between him and God. Other things had captured his mind—personal glory, the building of an empire, and an affair with another man's wife. Yet the long-ing for what he missed most led him to pray, "Create in me a clean heart, O God; and renew a right spirit within me" (Ps. 51:10, KJV). Joy can be ours again. The Lord is not so far away. Paul told the Philippians, "Rejoice in the Lord always; again I will say, Rejoice. . . . The Lord is at hand" (4:4-5).

In His last moments with His disciples Jesus said that He had spo-ken to them in order that His joy might be in them. He wants His divine and eternal joy to be in us and for our joy to be full. But it only comes in closeness with Him, and closeness with Jesus is in danger when we sin and turn away to other interests, or simply take Him for granted. Paul challenged the Philippians to "Rejoice in the Lord." Draw so close to Him that joy will be full and overflowing. Renew that powerful relationship. Revive that moment of joy when you first knew Him and realized His deep love for you.

Jesus said we have to be like little children to enter the kingdom of heaven. The very sight of her parents transforms a child who has been in day care or with a sitter all day. That little child, when she sees her parent, has a face transformed and beaming, and her joy cannot be contained. Arms wave, hands clap, and voice squeals as the child rushes into the arms of the one she loves. Yet, as the hours pass, the child becomes fussy, and the joy of the reunion fades.

Joy is a barometer of our relationship with people whom we some-times take for granted. Sadly, it is also a barometer of our relationship with the Lord who is with us every moment, yet is often taken for granted.

Joy comes as a gift from Christ, and it is experienced in nearness to Him. Joy is not isolated from the other attributes that describe the fruit of the Spirit. Christ declared to His disciples on the night that He was taken how they might share His joy:

> As the Father hath loved me, so have I loved you: continue ye in my love. If ye keep my commandments, ye shall abide in my love; even as I have kept my Father's commandments, and abide in his love. These things have I spoken unto you, that my joy might remain in you, and that your joy might be full (John 15:9-11, KJV).

**Notes**

1. Charles G. Finney, *Charles G. Finney: An Autobiography* (Old Tappan, N.J.: Fleming H. Revell, Co., n.d.), 20.

2. C. S. Lewis, *Surprised by Joy: The Shape of My Early Life* (New York: Harcourt, Brace, and Co., 1956), 237.

# 5 ||| Peace

The same night Jesus was taken by the soldiers of the high priest, He said something important about peace. In His last moments with the disciples in the upper room Jesus said, "Peace I leave with you; my peace I give to you; not as the world gives do I give to you. Let not your hearts be troubled, neither let them be afraid" (John 14:27).

People use the word *peace* in a variety of ways. In this last conversation with His disciples, however, Jesus took special care to distinguish between the varieties of peace that might be experienced. He took care to isolate what kind of peace the Spirit of God brings.

## Peace Related to Others

Often, people think of peace in terms of their relationship with other people. On the small scale, peace might relate to the people with whom we come in contact from day to day. On the large scale, peace becomes a matter of relationship between nations. War is the ultimate example of the absence of peace. Between individuals, fighting or arguing represents the absence of peace. Typically, peace means the absence of violence or conflict for most people.

A few years ago the relationship between the United States and the Soviet Union was described as "peaceful coexistence." Nikita Khrushchev enjoyed using the term. That relationship was also called the "cold war." The relationship between the two countries had an absence of killing, but there was an intense conflict marked by high anxiety over the threat of war: the possibility that war was just a button push away. I remember people building bomb shelters. I remember that we started digging one but were too lazy to finish. A family I knew had planned to put in a swimming pool, but instead they built a bomb shelter. High anxiety and fear of what might come marked the age.

In Jesus' time a comparable relationship existed between the Jews and Rome. The Roman Empire spread out and engulfed an area that included what had been the ancient kingdom of Israel. The Jews were not at war with Rome, but at the same time they were hardly at peace. An intense alienation existed between the Jews and the Roman army that occupied Judea. The temple represented the alienation in graphic terms with its inner court for the Jews and its outer court for the Gentiles. A decided mark, a line of demarcation, separated the two groups. Rudyard Kipling expressed the same sentiment in the opening lines of his poem "The Ballad of East and West": "Oh, East is East, and West is West, and never the twain shall meet."

Somehow we can persuade ourselves that some other person, or perhaps some other nation, is our enemy whether we are fighting or not. Anxiety and fear about that enemy haunts us every day. We even use terms such as "traditional enemies" in international relations. This term marked the attitude of the French and Germans toward one another for centuries. They were enemies as a matter of policy. The Irish and the English are traditional enemies. People become used to being enemies out of habit and practice. If traditional enemies are not currently killing each other, we may call that peace.

## Peace Related to Ourselves

Jesus told His disciples, however, that He was not giving peace the same way that the world gives it. His peace begins not with others but with ourselves. Peace is a dimension of spiritual life to be experienced within. The Jesus that promised His peace is the same Jesus who promised there would be war until He returned again. Therefore, His promise of peace was not a promise that there would be no conflict. His promise of peace was not a promise that there would be no war. Jesus did not define peace as the absence of conflict. We must face conflict all our lives; however, Jesus promised freedom from fear and anxiety in the face of that conflict.

Jesus said, "Let not your hearts be troubled" (John 14:1). Jesus meant for us to have the freedom to face conflict with a quiet resolve, knowing that what we do is right, even if it brings us into conflict with people.

The desire for freedom from anxiety has produced several major industries in the United States. People live with anxiety day in and day out in one way or another. Consider the advertisements on television for aspirin and pain medications. The drug industry thrives on offering something to relieve anxiety. It does not make the problem go away, but it claims to make the tension bearable. For many people, drinking provides a way of coping with anxiety. Alcohol does not make the source of the anxiety go away, but it seems to dull the pain.

Oddly enough, anxiety and fear actually lead to conflict at both the personal and international level. Our imaginations, or as Paul said in Galatians "our passions," flare up, and we wonder what people think about us. We wonder what someone has said about us. We wonder what people do when they are away from us. Our imaginations run wild. Our anxieties and fears take hold of us and actually create a state of conflict that marks the absence of peace.

In the book *The Camp of the Saints*, a French novelist has argued for the West to carry on a great war against Third World countries before they get too strong.[1] Fear compels this Frenchman to want to fight a war. His compulsion does not come from hatred but from fear. Hatred comes later as a by-product of fear, but fear and anxiety come first. Anxiety and fear tear us apart and create a cycle of increasing tension. The Hebrew word for peace speaks directly to the anxious condition of falling apart. The word *shalom* means literally "to be whole." We sometimes use the expression "pull yourself together." Pull all the parts back in place and be whole! An expression that developed among the hippies in the 1960s was "get your act together." Be at peace.

*Peace* was the name of the city-state over which the priest-king Melchizedek reigned: Salem. When David became king over Israel and conquered the old city of Salem to make it his capital, he changed its name to Jerusalem: God's Peace. Jesus said, "Let not your hearts be troubled, neither let them be afraid" (John 14:27). He said, "Do not be anxious about your life" (Matt. 6:25). But how does one do that? How does one go about not being anxious? How does one go about not being afraid? How does one stop worrying? It cannot be done on our own; something outside ourselves must intervene.

## Peace Related to God

In the Bible, peace comes as a by-product or a fringe benefit of our relationship with God. Twice, Isaiah wrote of peace "like a river."

(48:18; 66:12, KJV). Two hymns include the same phrase. In "It Is Well with My Soul," Horatio Spafford used the phrase to characterize the best moments of life and contrasted it with "sorrows like sea billows." In the old gospel hymn, having "peace like a river in my soul" is the well spring of joy and love. But what does it mean to have peace like a river? Like a river, peace must flow from some source. It is not self-generated. It comes from somewhere else, and it is moving. Peace comes to us from outside ourselves. Like a river, peace is not stagnant. It does not sit still like a pond. It constantly flows and constantly comes to us. It is not a one-time event that can be stored up and kept forever. It is dynamic.

Peace is not only the absence of the bad things of life. It is not just the absence of conflict, fighting, and war. Rather, peace is the presence of something good in the midst of the conflict. Something good flows into the middle of conflict. Conflict does not go away, but the good that flows in overwhelms it—the good is so much stronger and so much more powerful than the bad—that our spirits are left peaceful.

This understanding of peace like a river came to me in vivid terms on a blisteringly hot summer afternoon while I was preparing a sermon and reflecting on the phrase. In the course of preparing a sermon I usually "fling" myself all over the house before I am done. I had just flung myself across the bed, but all I could think of was how hot I was. The air-conditioning vent is right beside the bed, and as I was lying there only aware of how hot I was, suddenly the air conditioner clicked on, and the cool air began to rush over me. It was still one hundred degrees outside, and the relief I felt was not just the absence of the heat. Something replaced the heat. The cool air rushed over me and replaced the hot, stagnant air. I was overwhelmed by refreshment. How does this river of peace flow to us?

## How God Brings Peace

Isaiah indicated how the river of peace comes when he called the coming Savior the "Prince of Peace" (9:6). God began bringing us peace by taking the fear and anxiety out of religion. For uncountable centuries, religion seemed to exist to appease a god and keep that god from destroying us. Hollywood has popularized images of pagan rituals such as throwing young maidens into volcanoes to appease the gods. In fact, the image has a basis, because pagan religions were filled with constant fear and anxiety, wondering what the gods might do.

But in the Scriptures we find that the "Prince of Peace" came to abolish fear: "For in him all the fullness of God was pleased to dwell, and through him to reconcile to himself all things, whether on earth or in heaven, making peace by the blood of his cross" (Col. 1:19-20). Jesus Christ brought us God's peace so that we do not have to fear or be anxious about where we stand with God. We always know where we stand with God based on His promise. Because Jesus Christ came into the world to die for us, we know for a fact that God loves us. When we trust Him and believe that, we have full forgiveness. Peace begins with forgiveness. The Spirit of God is the river flowing through our lives that will give us peace in any situation.

Isaiah went on to say, "Thou wilt keep him in perfect peace, whose mind is stayed on thee: because he trusteth in thee" (26:3, KJV). Trusting God is the opening to peace. The Lord does not give us freedom from conflict. On the contrary, He often commands us to enter conflict. His peace is not the absence of that turmoil. His peace is His presence. His pulling us together is more than the absence of anxiety and fear. His presence comes in like that cool breeze to overwhelm and overshadow the cares that make for worry.

In the Old Testament an expression occurs over and over again when people were in tense situations. The Bible says the person "held his peace." How does one hold on to one's peace when a thousand worries or more would snatch it away? In terms of spiritual fruit, how does one bear the fruit of peace?

Having peace involves both pruning—taking away something—and fertilizing—adding something. Jesus said it all in the Sermon on the Mount. Cut out the anxiety and fear. Do not be anxious or worry about tomorrow. Tomorrow will have concerns enough without anticipating or imagining what they might be.

The fertilizing, or the positive effort that brings peace, also found expression in the Sermon on the Mount. Seek the kingdom of God and His righteousness. Practice the presence of the Lord in daily life. The promise of Jesus to His disciples was that He would be with them always. Many Christians accept His promise in theory but lose sight of His presence in the midst of all the worrisome happenings of life. It is impossible to concentrate on one's worries and think about the presence of the Lord at the same time. Persons can think about one or the other; they can flip-flop between the two, but they cannot think about both at the same time.

When we are preoccupied with Him, He overwhelms the fear and anxiety of anything we face. He puts all our passing worries in perspective. That last night, His closing words to them before He prayed were, "I have said this to you, that in me you may have peace. In the world you have tribulation; but be of good cheer, I have overcome the world" (John 16:33).

## Notes

1. Jean Raspail, *The Camp of the Saints*, trans. Norman Shapiro (Alexandria, Va.: The Institute for Western Values, 1982).

# 6 ||| Patience

Patience does not have the same delightful attraction of love, joy, and peace. The first three terms Paul uses to describe the quality of life in Christ seem somewhat beneficial; patience seems almost a penalty rather than a benefit. For many Christians, patience seems illusive and unattainable.

## Patience as Preparation

The Greek word *makrothumia* which translators have rendered as "patience" comes as a warning. The word is a bit of preparation for something to come, because this dimension of spiritual life can only be practiced and demonstrated in adversity, difficulty, or trying times. The term has been translated variously as patience, steadfastness, endurance, forbearance, and long-suffering. In essence, it involves the long, patient endurance of injuries, insults, and other troubles.

Jesus spoke about many of the qualities of spiritual life marking the fruit of the Spirit on that last night with His disciples in the upper room. After He had warned them of coming tribulation and things they must endure from family and friends as well as enemies, He said, "I have said these things to you, that when their hour comes you may remember that I told you of them" (John 16:4). The word *patience* reminds Christians of this warning from Jesus.

To say patience is one of the dimensions of spiritual life that results from the indwelling of the Holy Spirit is to say troubles will come in every Christian's life which will require the durability that comes from this quality. As He gathered with His disciples for the last time, Jesus warned them of coming troubles. The last chance Jesus had to talk with His disciples, He devoted to preparing them for hardship.

### Denial—Refusing to Prepare

Amazingly enough, sometimes people simply refuse to be prepared. We would rather not know; we would rather not even think that something unpleasant might happen. In his spiritual autobiography *Surprised by Joy,* C. S. Lewis spoke of the thing he dreaded most in his early years—going back to school. Brought up in the English public school tradition, Lewis went away to school for three months at a time. For Lewis, leaving home to go to school was a dreadful thing. When vacation came, it was so glorious he preferred to think that it would never end.

Lewis exhibited the intellectual and emotional struggle people often have. Intellectually, we may know that tragedy comes to all people, but emotionally we say, "Ah, but it happens to other people, not to me!" Lewis preferred not to think that his vacation would ever come to an end. As a result, he was never prepared emotionally when the time came for him to go back to school again.

We often try to think of tragedy as something that happens to other people, but never to us. As a result, we are seldom prepared when tragedy or trouble comes. Jesus warns us, however, because He wants His disciples to know that injury, insult, and trouble will come to us. For Christians the question arises, "How will I respond when trouble comes?"

*Ostrich Theology*

People respond to trouble in a variety of ways. One of the most common is denial. This might be called "ostrich theology." Ostriches bury their heads in the sand, and if they cannot see trouble, it is not there. In the same way, people refuse to see the troubles that might surround them. People who deal with trouble in this way expect that if they ignore the problem long enough it will go away. Some people believe this approach shows spiritual strength. Denial of reality, however, is not the same thing as faith. In faith, one must first admit that something is wrong before relief can come.

While serving as a prison chaplain, I learned something about denial. The counselor, who worked with sex offenders ranging from rapists to child molesters, had a requirement for anyone who wanted to be in the therapy group. The counselor required the prisoners to admit their guilt. An amazing number of people in prison will not admit their guilt. The rationale for the requirement was that someone who was not a sex offender had no business in a therapy group for sex offenders. But more to the point, a person who would not admit something was wrong would not be willing to do anything about the problem. This therapy group in prison has its parallel in everyday life as well. Those who will not face the reality of difficulty in their lives will never do anything about the problem. They will continue to bury their heads in the sand.

Denial ranks among the most popular ways of dealing with trouble. Denial forms the whole background for Buddhist thought. Buddhists hold that the material world does not exist. Christian Scientists share this view and believe that sin involves acting as though a material world does exist. In such a mind-set, trouble cannot exist because nothing exists that can cause trouble. The appearance of trouble, pain, or suffering must be ignored lest the idea develop that a real world exists in which people suffer.

*Fantasy*

One man in prison will always come to mind when I think of this subject. He had become involved in a gnostic cult known as The Way, and he believed he was a spiritual being no longer subject to the laws of nature. Whenever I inquired as to his health, the prisoner always replied, "Everything is beautiful!" No matter what had happened to him that day, whether he had been beaten up in the dormitory or just received a setback from the parole board, the man always gave the same answer. As he spoke he smiled a painful smile, trying to convince himself that everything was beautiful.

Blanche Du Bois took this approach in Tennessee Williams's play *A Street Car Named Desire.* She had lost everything including a fiancée, a plantation, and her reputation. Yet, she managed to build herself a fantasy world in which everything was beautiful. Blanche still saw herself a great lady. She still believed she was courted by handsome, intelligent, wealthy suitors. She lost her mind. She so deeply denied the unpleasantness in her life, that she lost all contact with life.

## Acceptance—Prelude to Despair

While denial leads to disaster, acceptance is not necessarily any better. Sometimes when people accept their situations, they not only accept and face the reality of the trouble and trials they are going through, but they go one step farther and accept defeat. Acceptance offers no solution when in the same moment one accepts defeat because defeat leads inevitably to despair.

### Defeat

Sometimes the hardest thing for people to see is an option. Defeat may have an alternative. People who decide to attempt suicide may do so because they think they have viewed life's problems and decided they have no options: "I am defeated, my troubles have overcome me, and I have no way out." When we confront the difficulties of life and decide we have no hope, we accept defeat.

Defeat and despair pose one of the greatest problems for modern urban life. As life becomes more and more complicated in the technological age of instant communication, a feeling grows that we have no control over our own lives. When we feel that we have no control, stress also builds and builds. Through stress, people can inflict a form of suffering on themselves that leads to the acceptance of defeat and despair.

### Futility

Anyone who has ever tried to deal with a bureaucratic institution knows the kind of powerlessness and futility that can come from that experience. Whether from a government institution or the job we hold, the ordinary frustrations of daily life can train us to accept defeat. People even find that they have no control over their own personal schedules and private time. A growing feeling that we have lost control of our own lives permeates society. Losing control helps create that sense of helplessness that marks despair.

When people accept their lot, despair takes over. With a shrug of the shoulders, some habitually respond to the trials of life, "Well, that's the way things will be, there's nothing I can do about it, and I might as well give up." This surrender to despair can hold people in bondage throughout their lives, because it is learned early.

People begin assigning labels to individuals at an early age. You are ignorant. You are an unmanageable child. You are no good. You are stupid. With all the thousands of labels people are willing to tag on us, how many do we despairingly accept as reality? Acceptance is not necessarily better than denial.

People will often simply decide to fail. Failure may seem simpler than the struggle. In his monumental work *A Study of History,* Arnold Toynbee was trying to decide what made great civilizations emerge. In his quest, Toynbee investigated not only the places where great civilizations emerged but also the places where civilization did not develop beyond a primitive state. He studied the Eskimos as well as the Romans. Toynbee noticed something about difficulty. Where people accepted suffering as the normal way of life, taking for granted the harshness and difficulty, they gave up the hope that there might be some alternative.

When the Eskimos crossed the land bridge from Siberia ages ago, they faced a series of dense forests. They had no tools for cutting the trees or clearing the land. Going into the forests seemed too great a difficulty. It seemed hopeless. Rather than move into the forests and on down the continent as the ancestors of the great Indian civilizations did, the Eskimos stayed where they were in the frozen wastelands of the north. They did not hope for anything better than that, so they capitulated to the difficulty.

Job's wife gave the same advice. When everything bad that could possibly happen had happened, Job's wife told him to curse God and die. She saw no hope for Job. He might as well accept defeat and be done with it.

We experience a tension when we face great trials. Defeat has a natural attraction because at least it brings a kind of end. Any ending will do; just let it all be over. There is a pull to accept defeat in the face of pain, trouble, and adversity of all kinds. Israel felt this pull in the wilderness. No sooner had they left Egypt and begun to make their way through the wilderness than they began to lament that it was better for them in Egypt. They argued it was better to have remained as slaves than to die in the desert (Ex. 16:3). Israel decided that defeat was better than the trouble they were going through.

## Hope—The Grounds for Patience

Somewhere between denial and despair lies hope. Somewhere in that region where we honestly recognize and admit the trouble that faces us, and where we decide that we will get through it, this word *makrothumia* emerges. Patient endurance! What makes for endurance or durability?

I once bought a wallet by mail. A credit card company offered the wallet as a special deal for its customers, and I fell for it lock, stock, and barrel. It looked like a super wallet. It had a pen with a digital clock on the end of it. It had a small calculator for me to figure out how deeply in debt I stayed. It had a place for my checkbook, so I could spend my life away. It had a note pad for me to write memos to myself. It could hold dozens of credit cards. It even had a place for me to keep money. It was truly a super wallet.

The wallet began falling apart a week after I got it. The spring in the pen broke, but that did not matter because it did not write anyway. The calculator flashed off and on in the middle of a calculation. Some numbers worked, and others did not. The binding tore when I folded it. The super wallet, as grand as it seemed, had no durability. What makes for endurance or durability? Some people are not unlike that wallet when it comes to durability.

The company that made the wallet was not particularly interested in making a wallet that would last. They were interested in selling wallets. As soon as this wallet had given its all, I had to buy another wallet. Planned obsolescence is a part of the American system. There is such a thing as planned survival, too.

### Planned Survival

In planned survival, we can decide that we are going to survive. We can decide that we are going to get through our difficulties. We can decide, in contrast to Israel, that we can get through the wilderness to the Promised Land.

A few years ago, Great Britain was going through one of its periodic crises. It may have been a labor dispute, an economic problem, or an international crisis. The nature of the problem is unimportant. In the midst of a discussion of the problem someone was criticizing the British and prophesying that they would never get through this crisis. At that point my father interjected a comment about the British. He had been with them during the blitz in London, and he had fought beside them in France, Belgium, and Germany. He said, "The British are survivors."

In speeches to the people during the Second World War, Winston Churchill continually urged the people toward hope. Years later after the war, Churchill addressed the boys of one of Britain's public schools. Reflecting on the struggles and difficulties he had faced, he offered this advice, "Never give up, never, never, never, never."

People can decide that they will endure through any crisis and emerge on the other side. In the study of civilization, when Arnold Toynbee began to examine why some civilizations do endure, he looked at Britain—a tiny little island cut off from the rest of Europe—with a storm-tossed sea around it, a rugged countryside that will not grow very much food, and a people of often contrary independence. Why would it become the ruler of one of the greatest empires the world has ever known? When the British see difficulty, trial, and trouble, they do not see it as defeat. They see it as opportunity.

Pain, trouble, insult, injury, and all manners of adversity will all happen to us at some time or another, Jesus insisted, but we can make a decision about how we will respond to them. Like the Unsinkable Molly Brown sang in the Broadway play, "I may be low, but I'm not down yet."

## Looking Beyond Trouble

We can look beyond our troubles. If the spirit of Christ dwells within us, we cannot be defeated. The Spirit of Christ is a Spirit of durability or endurance that shares the power to endure with our spirits. Instead of fearing what lies ahead, Christians can go forward with the assurance that they can endure, "for God did not give us a spirit of timidity but a spirit of power" (2 Tim. 1:7). The real presence and power of the Holy Spirit in our lives is the basis for endurance. Without the confident assurance of that presence and power, people have no real basis for hope.

Despite all his other suffering, Job's greatest anguish came because he was not sure of God's presence in the suffering. He railed against his friends and argued with them, but Job's most dramatic statements came from his longing for certainty of God's presence:

"Oh, that I knew where I might find him,
that I might come even to his seat!
Behold, I go forward, but he is not there;
and backward, but I cannot perceive him;
on the left hand I seek him, but I cannot behold him;
I turn to the right hand, but I cannot see him" (23:3,8-9).

Endurance comes in the presence of Christ who brings the knowledge that something lies ahead, that we have a future, and that we can look forward to it with hope.

The fruit of the Spirit of Christ describes what the life of a person is like when Jesus Christ dwells in that life. The fruit of the Spirit results from a Christian taking on the character of Christ. The fruit of the Spirit is the natural result of being in Christ. Whatever Christ's character is like, our character is becoming "from one degree of glory to another; for this comes from the Lord who is the Spirit" (2 Cor. 3:18).

Yet a Christian must consciously cooperate with Christ in order to experience the patient endurance He offers. At the conclusion of the Sermon on the Mount, Jesus told the story of a man who built his house on a rock, "and the rain fell, and the floods came, and the winds blew and beat upon that house, but it did not fall, because it had been founded on the rock" (Matt. 7:25). Jesus said this foundation came from hearing His words and doing them (v. 24).

*Sharing Christ's Durability*

Christians can endure suffering, pain, insult, injury, and affliction because Christ did. His Spirit dwells within all believers. The Bible says that Christ "for the joy that was set before him endured the cross" (Heb. 12:2). Jesus' durability allowed Him to endure the cross and come to believers as a gift by virtue of the presence of His Spirit in their lives. Beyond the suffering of the cross lay the victory of the resurrection. In Paul's great prayer for believers in the first chapter of Ephesians, he prayed that we might know the hope that God offers, the riches we have already inherited, and "the immeasurable greatness of his power in us who believe, according to the working of his great might which he accomplished in Christ when he raised him from the dead." (Eph. 1:19-20). The same power that brought Christ through the misery of the cross to the glory of the resurrection is at work in everyone who believes on Christ!

Suffering holds no virtue. It has nothing to commend itself. Martin Luther discovered that fact when he searched for God in his own life. Luther thought that if he tormented his body enough by beating himself, wrapping himself in chains, wearing a hair shirt, and in other ways punishing himself, that the suffering would somehow bring him to the Lord. Of course, Luther only succeeded in increasing his anguish. After he knew the Lord loved him, had died for him, and had extended mercy to him personally, however, Luther found that he could endure anything:

> The Spirit and the gifts are ours
> Thro' Him who with us sideth:
> Let goods and kindred go,
> This mortal life also;
> The body they may kill:
> God's truth abideth still,
> His kingdom is forever.[1]

Suffering is not desirable, but Christians can rejoice through their suffering because they have hope that something better lies beyond the immediate moment of gloom.

## Notes

1. Martin Luther, "A Mighty Fortress Is Our God," *Baptist Hymnal* (Nashville: Convention Press, 1975), 37.

# 7 ||| Kindness

Like endurance, kindness becomes a possibility only when some other option could be chosen. Just as endurance only becomes a possibility during adversity, kindness only becomes a possibility when someone could be other than kind. Being unkind is the rather obvious alternative to kindness. Kindness is also a quality that can only be manifest in relation to other people. Kindness cannot be shown solitarily.

## Kindness as an Option

As I sit at my desk in my study preparing for a sermon or studying the Scriptures, kindness is not an active dimension of my spirit. When the telephone rings and interrupts me eight times in the course of an hour, however, I have the opportunity of showing kindness. "Are you busy?" they ask.

"I'm studying," I reply. Then they continue talking because studying does not constitute being busy to them. I could respond indignantly, "Toad! Don't bother me when I'm studying." I have that option. People can only be kind when they have the option to be something else.

This word *kindness* which Paul uses in Galatians to describe the fruit of the Spirit is often linked with the quality of patience. Kindness has a relationship to the quality of life marked by endurance, forebearance, and long-suffering. In 1 Corinthians 13, Paul says that charity is long-suffering and kind. These two qualities are essential ingredients of the other quality—charity. All of the qualities which describe the fruit of the Spirit have a mutual dependence and interrelatedness about them. They weave together like a fabric. Several other passages in the New Testament link kindness with the concept of endurance or long-suffering. Paul mentions the relationship again in 2 Corinthians

6:6 and Colossians 3:12.

Kindness has its greatest opportunity for expression in difficult situations. At those times, people have the greatest temptation to to be unkind; therefore, they have the greatest opportunity to show kindness. When a well-meaning individual ruins plans and efforts we have labored over by simply sticking his or her nose where it does not belong, how do we handle it? When we are under great stress to complete a job or when pressures of work and life problems mount, how do we treat the people who, through no fault of their own, are around us? In a thousand difficult situations of life, we have the option of showing kindness.

## Kindness—What God Is Like

Jesus said that kindness is what God is like. We show that we are legitimate children of the Most High when we act kindly because God is kind to even the ungrateful and the selfish. Kindness is the way God treats the human race. Jesus said, "Love your enemies, and do good, and lend, expecting nothing in return; and your reward will be great, and you will be sons of the Most High; for he is kind to the ungrateful and the selfish" (Luke 6:35). Kindness is the way God has always related to people. Kindness is an essential aspect of God's nature and forms the basis for people being kind. Paul repeats the theme: "Be kind to one another, tenderhearted, forgiving one another, as God in Christ forgave you" (Eph. 4:32). In considering the fruit of the Spirit, we need to recall that the fruit does not come from the human spirit but from the Holy Spirit. The qualities that distinguish the fruit of the Spirit are characteristics of God the Holy Spirit. The fruit of the Spirit is what God is like.

### Kindness to the Unworthy

Kindness is one of God's distinguishing characteristics, and Jesus told His disciples to be like God who is kind to the ungrateful and the selfish. Kindness and being kind are not based on someone's worthiness to receive kindness. God shows kindness because that is what He is like, not because people are so worthy that they elicit kindness from Him. On the contrary, God's kindness shows itself in spite of the way people are.

Kindness is like love in the sense that it should not be shown just to people who deserve it. When people deserve kindness, they have earned the right to be treated in a particular way. In this case, nice treatment is a reward or compensation for an acceptable form of behavior. Nice treatment is exchanged as a matter of routine behavior between friends, family, and social equals.

## More Than Doing Good

Kindness comes out when someone has the real possibility of being other than kind. Kindness involves more, however, than merely doing nice things. It is possible to do a nice thing or a good deed without being kind. The welfare system in the United States does good things but not necessarily in a kind way. Sometimes the welfare system does its work in a way that may destroy self-respect and personal dignity.

Any bureaucratic structure can succumb to this flaw of the welfare system, whether it be the Internal Revenue Service, the army, the school board, or the admissions office of a hospital. Any institution that becomes big enough faces the danger of losing interest in treating people kindly. Such structures become task oriented, not people oriented. Like these structures, people may also do good things without necessarily being kind. In the Bible, kindness has a necessary relationship to compassion as it does in Colossians where believers are exhorted to, "Put on then, as God's chosen ones, holy and beloved, compassion, kindness" (Col. 3:12). Compassion, caring, and concern for people are dimensions of kindness.

## Confrontation

Sometimes a sense of compassion can lead people to think that kindness means avoiding difficulty, controversy, or confrontation with unworthy people. The most kind thing to do in such situations, however, may be to confront the person. The greatest demonstration of concern for someone's welfare does not come in avoidance but in facing the difficulty squarely. Kindness and compassion serve as the arena in which the confrontation takes place.

Jesus serves as a model for this kind of confrontation. A rich young ruler came to Jesus and asked, "Teacher, what must I do to inherit eternal life?"

Jesus said, "You know the commandments."

"Yes, of course," the young man replied, "All these I have observed from my youth."

Then Mark makes the comment that Jesus *loved* him and said, "You lack one thing" (10:21). The confrontation came, based on the fact that Jesus loved the young man. He kindly told the young man to sell all that he had and give to the poor, and he would have riches in heaven. The young man went away sad because he had great riches. The confrontation came out of kindness, based on compassion.

### Living the Kindness of God

Kindness is a difficult thing to do. But if kindness is a characteristic of God, and the Holy Spirit dwells within us, then kindness ought to be a characteristic of our lives. The Bible says to "put on" kindness (Col. 3:12). It is something that can be decided upon and done, just like putting on a coat. And like a coat, kindness is what people see on the outside. Kindness shows if it is present.

The *King James Version* of the Bible sometimes translates the word under discussion as "goodness." The Greek language had two major words for goodness. One carries the idea of "being good." The word under discussion, however, does not include the moral or ethical idea. Instead, it involves being useful or serviceable. It means "being good for something" or "doing good." In relation to people it entails doing good or being kind to them.

The same idea lies behind the word God used to evaluate creation. When God surveyed all that He had made, He declared that it was good. He did not mean that it did not break the law. He did not mean that the sun neither lies nor cheats. He did not mean creation is ethical. He was saying that His creation did what it was created to do. It was being what it was created to be.

The same standard applies to people. God created people to do good to one another, that is called kindness. Just as God looked at creation and saw that it was good, He also looks at us. The prophet Micah said, "He hath showed thee, O man, what is good" (Mic. 6:8). God has an intention and purpose for what people should be and how they should act toward one another. God has something in mind for the human race, and that purpose is the measuring stick by which God evaluates us.

Too often it is easier to hurt someone's feelings than to be kind. It may be easier to see someone's faults than to see his or her needs. One of the leading maxims of life inside the prisons is "kindness is weakness." When circumstances create the opportunity to be kind, they also create the option to do something else. They create the opportunity to exercise strength and power over someone else. When we have the option to be kind, our other option is to hurt.

Exercising power gives us a sense of self-fulfillment. Power feeds that maddening human thirst to be like God. How ironic that Jesus said we become like God in weakness rather than in strength. "But love your enemies, and do good, and lend, expecting nothing in return; and your reward will be great, and you will be sons of the Most High; for he is kind to the ungrateful and the selfish" (Luke 6:35).

When I was young, my Sunday School class was full of nice boys from nice families. A little fellow came to our class for awhile. He looked a little gawky, and he was very poor. His parents did not come to church, but they lived in the neighborhood of the church on the "other side of the highway," down where everyone changed apartments regularly, and no one stayed too long. His clothes were not in style in those days, when a boy had to wear a Madras shirt and Weejun moccasins to face the world. We found that it was fun to make fun of that little boy. He had come to church on his own, wanting to know about Jesus, and we drove him away. I do not know what ever happened to that boy. We had the opportunity to be kind to someone who could never do anything for us. We chose to be cruel. People have a great capacity for cruelty.

Jesus said that those who want to be children of God should just be chips off the old block. God is kind. The fruit of the Spirit includes kindness, because "like Father, like son."

# 8 ||| Goodness

When I was a little boy, my mother taught me to pray, "God is great, God is good, and we thank Thee for this food." This simple prayer makes a simple statement about God, yet it is remarkably profound and sophisticated in the depth of its theology. God is not only great, but God is good. This kind of goodness goes beyond the functional, pragmatic goodness discussed in the last chapter. It involves moral goodness.

## God Is Good

The idea that God is good has been the object of speculation and debate for centuries upon centuries. The Greek philosophers argued about the nature of goodness thousands of years ago. Socrates, Plato, Euripides, and Aristotle all contemplated and argued and tried to decide what constitutes "the good." They also wanted to know how a person knows what is good. Discerning goodness was as important for them as describing goodness.

### The Standard for Goodness: What Is Good?

The debate inevitably leads to the question of whether or not some universal standard or ideal exists whereby God may be judged to be good. How does a person decide whether or not God is good, and what standard is used in determining it? If such a standard exists for judging God, and if such a standard can be perceived and understood, then that standard or ideal or principle would be greater than God. It would be the judge of God. It would be the God of God.

Christian ethicists have argued whether or not God submits to a moral code of behavior. Such a code would keep God in line and let God know what can and cannot be done. It would be a way for God to know good and evil. It would be a guide to instruct God's decision-making. It would help ensure that God would do what was expected of Him. Such a code or principle or ideal would imply that God is capable of evil. Is there a universal principle to which even God submits?

Jesus addressed this question point blank. Without dealing with any of the turns and twists of the argument or the subtleties of the debate, Jesus gave a simple dogmatic answer: "Behold, one came up to him, saying, 'Teacher, what good deed must I do, to have eternal life?' And he said to him, 'Why do you ask me about *what* is good? One there is *who* is good' " (Matt. 19:16-17, author's italics).

The young man asked for a standard. He wanted the comfort of a moral code. If Jesus would provide a list of what constituted goodness, he could take care of the rest. The question the young man asked was taking him away from the thing he sought. He looked for goodness in terms of a standard or principle. He looked for a *what* instead of a *who*.

### The Nature of Goodness: Who Is Good?

Mark recorded the same or similar encounter in the Gospel. His account stresses another dimension of the great debate:

> As he was setting out on his journey, a man ran up, knelt before him, and asked, "Good Teacher, what must I do to inherit eternal life?" And Jesus said to him, "Why do you call *me* good? No one is good but God alone" (Mark 10:17-18).

Jesus insisted that the young man clarify in his mind the only circumstance under which Jesus might be called good. If Jesus was only a famous teacher, then He had no right to be called good. If Jesus was only a well-known and prominent rabbi, then He had no right to be called good. He did not want flattery. Only one being in all of existence is morally good, and that being is God. Moral goodness is a unique attribute of God. No other person and no other thing is morally good.

In Matthew, Jesus stressed that things are not good. No principle or ideal of goodness exists independently of God. Only God is good. In Mark, Jesus stressed that people are not good. No matter how great teachers may be, they are not good. Only God is good. Goodness is a unique characteristic of who God is. Goodness is a quality of God that only exists because God exists.

Through His exchange with the young man, Jesus sought to help the young man understand whom he was addressing and what goodness had to do with Him. Jesus was good for a special reason. Jesus shared life with the Father. Goodness was an essential part of Jesus because of His relationship to God. He was not good because of the good deeds He did. Jesus did good deeds because He was good. It was His nature; the nature He shared with God. It is this nature that He came to share with people.

The young man was engaged in an exercise in futility, trying to be good by doing good deeds. A bad tree cannot bear good fruit. A good tree cannot help but bear good fruit. That is its nature (Matt. 7:17-18).

Goodness does not come by knowing what is good. Goodness in a person does not result from the careful arrival at a code of behavior. Goodness begins in knowing God. What God does and what God says is what goodness is. Goodness is shown by God in His activity. Goodness, then, is not an ideal standard for evaluating God; rather, God is the standard for understanding goodness.

## The Knowledge of Good and Evil

Since the beginning of time, however, it has been the human habit to determine values independently of God. The problem goes back to Adam and Eve as they desired to be like God. The serpent dangled a fascinating idea before them—the promise that they would know good and evil, just like God. The idea caught their fancy, and they ate the fruit of the tree of knowledge in order to know good and evil. Then their eyes were open to good and evil. In this act of sin, their relationship with God was broken.

God is the source of wisdom, understanding, and truth. Adam and Eve had none of these. Throughout the Bible, God reveals the problem of having knowledge without wisdom, understanding, and truth. The absence of these ingredients makes even knowledge invalid. This was the charge that God laid on Job: "Who is this that darkens counsel by words without knowledge?" (Job 38:2). In Nineveh the same problem arose because the people did not know "their right hand from their left" (Jonah 4:11).

## Goodness Is More Than Knowledge

Goodness involves more than mere knowledge. It requires more than a factual understanding of a moral code. A person may have a thorough knowledge of an ethical system and still be an evil person. Jesus asked the young man who came to Him if he knew the commandments, and the young man did. That knowledge did not make him good. A person may also do good deeds and still be an evil person. Evil people are capable of doing good deeds. The young man who came to Jesus had done the good deeds of the Law, but the deeds did not make him good.

Goodness involves more than our knowledge or our actions. It goes down deep to our very nature. Goodness is an essential ingredient of a person, like blood and bone, or it is not present at all. The knowledge of good and evil does nothing to affect our nature. Knowledge is just the playground in which people act out what they are really like.

For example, a person may know it is wrong to steal. For four years I served as chaplain in a prison full of men who knew it was wrong to steal. Their problem had not been one of ignorance or misinformation. They had knowledge, but that knowledge had no affect on them. Many of the men at the prison knew it was wrong to rape, but that knowledge had not affected their lives. Any number of crimes can be cataloged in which people knew their actions were wrong but performed the acts in spite of their knowledge.

## The Failure of Human Nature

Since goodness involves something other than a mere legal code or moral code, the failure of knowledge to bring goodness can also be witnessed in places other than in prisons. Not all failures of goodness are categorized as human crimes. Of the fifteen works of the flesh that Paul mentions in Galatians 5:19-21, none are considered crimes in modern America. The knowledge of these bad things and others like them does little to diminish their occurrence. "Nice" people may know what they ought to do and still not do it, even if they want to do it.

This failure of human nature was the great lament of Paul in the seventh chapter of Romans. He had knowledge of the moral will of God. He knew the Law, and the Law revealed the righteousness of

God. The young man who came to Jesus had the same knowledge, but he had not reached the point of Paul, who knew he was not living totally in the righteousness of God. Paul had the knowledge, but it did him no good. He was not able to do the good he wanted to do! He cried out about his dilemma:

> I do not understand my own actions. For I do not do what I want, but I do the very thing I hate. Now if I do what I do not want, I agree that the law is good. So then it is no longer I that do it, but sin which dwells within me. For I know that nothing good dwells within me, that is, in my flesh. I can will what is right, but I cannot do it. For I do not do the good I want, but the evil I do not want is what I do (Rom. 7:15-19).

Paul made an important qualification, that goodness does not dwell "in my flesh." It is not a part of the natural human animal. Paul had come face-to-face with the failure of the human will and the failure of human nature. He recognized that goodness is something different from what people are. Goodness eludes us, even when we crave it.

### Settling for Less

As a result, people have tended to settle for something less than the goodness they crave. We have made goodness a relative idea so that something is good compared to something else. We can compare ourselves with others and come up looking pretty good. If we compare Franklin Roosevelt to Adolf Hitler, Roosevelt looks good. On the other hand, a Republican might compare Roosevelt with Herbert Hoover and prefer Hoover. Of course, a Democrat probably would not share that opinion.

Everything becomes relative when placed on a human level. On that level, goodness ceases to be an absolute eternal quality and becomes merely a way of saying what we like. If I like something, it is good. If I do not like it, it is bad. So it is not a universal ideal which we want to tell us what constitutes goodness. In the end, people want to be the judges.

This trap of settling for something less snares many people. It can even snare Christians when they let themselves become judges of what is good and what is bad. The excuse for avoiding Christian fellowship, worship, and servant responsibilities sounds similar to the excuse given for never becoming a Christian: "I am just as good as they are."

First of all, the excuse is true. I eagerly agree anytime I hear that excuse given. I heartily agree every time I hear a nominal Christian give that excuse for not becoming a part of the body of believers gathered in a local church.

Unfortunately, that excuse is the bad news. To be just as good as everybody else is a confession of guilt, sin, and need. If we are only as good as everybody else, we are in deep need, as Paul understood. If we are as good as everybody else, we stand in a hopeless position:

> "None is righteous, no, not one;
> no one understands, no one seeks for God.
> All have turned aside, together they have gone wrong;
> no one does good, not even one" (Rom. 3:10-12).

What an easy standard we set when we ask to be as good as everybody else. It sounds like my physical fitness schedule. I walk to work at least once a week. I live only a hundred yards from my office, but I manage to reach my standard. Unfortunately, my standard does me no good.

## Sharing God's Goodness

This situation leaves people in a curious quandary. If no one is good, how can goodness be something God expects of us? It does not seem fair, somehow.

### Becoming Children of God

Perhaps the solution to the quandary lies in the passage in which the word *goodness* is found. It is described by Paul as being one of the characteristics of the fruit of the Spirit. The fruit is something that the Spirit produces, and goodness is one thing that can be said of the life that the Spirit produces. Just as an apple tree produces one kind of fruit, the Spirit of God produces one kind of fruit: children of God.

Though an apple tree produces only one kind of fruit, many things may describe that fruit when it is fully mature. An apple may be round, red, firm, juicy, sweet, tart, and crisp. The different characteristics are all part of the essential nature of an apple. In the same way, Paul gave a number of terms to describe the result of the Holy Spirit in a human life. *Goodness* is one of these. The fruit of the Spirit is not the manifestation of our human nature. It is not produced by the human spirit. The human spirit is a part of what Paul calls the flesh. The fruit of the Spirit begins to come about as a result of a divine transformation of a person. We become something that we were not before, and the Holy Spirit begins to produce something different in our lives that we could never produce before. Goodness is one of those things.

## A Change of Nature

In describing this transformation, Paul sounds like he may have just returned from a retreat with the beloved disciple John who was so fond of speaking in terms of light and darkness. Paul wrote to the Ephesians: "For once you were darkness, but now you are light in the Lord; walk as children of light (for the fruit of light is found in all that is good and right and true)" (5:8-9). When we become children of God, we are changed by His Spirit which is at work in us. God is making His children good. When His Holy Spirit enters the life of a believer, the person begins to take on the character of that new life because goodness is a unique characteristic of God.

When people become believers in the Lord Jesus Christ, God changes them into a new kind of life form! The change is not just a change in legal status—that one's guilt is forgiven. Jesus said a believer would be born from above by the Holy Spirit (John 3:6-7). Faith does not give a person a fresh start as a human but a fresh start as an immortal child of God because "if any one is in Christ, he is a new creation; the old has passed away, behold, the new has come" (2 Cor. 5:17). When this change comes about, God begins to transform the human character until it conforms to His own (2 Cor. 3:18). The Book of Acts describes Barnabas as "a good man, full of the Holy Spirit" (Acts 11:24). Goodness came as a result of the fullness of the Spirit in his life.

Goodness does not come forth in a life as a result of knowing a theoretical, philosophical system. Goodness does not come about by knowing a code of ethics or a statement of laws. It does not come about by doing what we deem to be good deeds. Goodness only comes about by knowing God and letting Him have His way with us.

Goodness is a matter of becoming like Jesus. It happens naturally for those who set their minds and their hearts on Christ. The only possible way for Christians not to be filled with goodness is to set their minds on the passions and desires of the flesh rather than on Christ.

The rich, young man who came to Jesus had his bag full of passions and desires. He had his mind full of presuppositions and judgments about God. The saddest moment in his life came when Jesus gave him a straight answer. Everything he thought that he knew about goodness was wrong. Not only that, but he had to decide between his own passions and what God wanted for him. So Jesus made him an offer, If you want to go to heaven and be perfect, go on, get rid of all that junk, and come along with Me; I'm going to heaven soon.

# 9 ||| Faith

On the eve of the most devastating event in the history of the world, Jesus told His disciples to have faith in Him: "Ye believe in God, believe also in me" (John 14:1, KJV). When the guards took Jesus away and the authorities put Him to death, however, the disciples fled in terror. They witnessed the events and believed their Master was defeated. They failed to understand that in the midst of what appeared to be defeat, Christ was the victor. Sin, death, Satan, and the powers of evil were totally vanquished. Unfortunately, the disciples trusted their senses instead of the Lord.

Faith has a grasp of reality which the senses alone cannot supply. While the world holds that "seeing is believing," the Bible points toward a reality which is perceived "by faith, not by sight" (2 Cor. 5:7). Faith may operate independently of the senses, or it may operate in defiance of the senses! More than simple a form of knowledge, faith is the spiritual quality that interprets and assigns meaning and value to all other forms of knowledge. Faith in Jesus Christ governs how one will react to every other fact or event in the universe. Jesus told His disciples to believe in Him because that belief or faith would form the basis for anything else that might follow. Without faith, they could not receive what He wanted to give to them. In those last moments with them around the table and before He went into the garden to pray, Jesus exhorted His closest friends to have faith in Him. Each time He exhorted them to faith, He gave a promise of what faith in Him would make possible.

In John 14:1-7, Jesus explains that faith is the way one receives eternal life. In John 14:8-17, Jesus explains that faith is the basis for access to God through prayer. Whereas acceptance of what Jesus said forms an aspect of faith, belief in the ideas He taught is not the focus of faith.

Jesus did not call for His disciples to believe the ideas so much as He called for them to believe Him. What Jesus taught becomes believable only if one has faith in Jesus.

### Faith as Response

Abraham holds a unique place in the Bible. Because of his faith in God, he became the father of the people to whom God entrusted the oracles and the written Word (Rom. 3:2; Heb. 1:1). He stands as a prime example of faith. All of the Gospels refer to Abraham in his special role as the father of the Jews. He is also mentioned by Paul, James, Peter, and the author of Hebrews. Christians, Jews, and Muslims all acknowledge Abraham.

Abraham's virtue, however, did not lie in believing in the existence of God. Adam and Eve believed in God enough to want to be just like Him. They had firsthand, personal experience with God. Cain believed in God enough to worship Him and offer sacrifices to Him. The people of the earth believed in God enough to build a tower that would reach all the way to heaven. While people may be sinful by nature, they are also religious by nature (Acts 17:22; Rom. 1:25). Abraham's faith involved more than simple belief that God exists.

Belief in the existence of God has nothing much to commend it if that belief has no effect on a person. It corresponds to the parable of the talents (Matt. 25:14-30). Three servants are given different sums of money to administer in the absence of their master. When the master returns, he finds that two of the servants handled their money well, but the third servant did absolutely nothing with his. The anger of the master focuses on the fact that the servant knew the master well enough to have done something:

> "You wicked and slothful servant! You knew that I reap where I have not sowed, and gather where I have not winnowed? Then you ought to have invested my money with the bankers, and at my coming I should have received what was my own with interest" (Matt. 25:26-27).

For all his knowledge of the master, the servant behaved as though the master did not exist. Belief is not so much an act of the intellect as it is an act of the will. As such Christ can command us: "Believe in God, believe also in me" (John 14:1).

Faith is the way a person reacts to the body of information found in the Bible. Faith is the way one interprets that information and assigns meaning to it. Faith does more than say, "This information is true." Faith causes a change in behavior because this information demands a response. The sophisticated cigarette smoker may regard the surgeon general's warning on the cigarette pack as true without ever submitting to that truth. Each bit of truth in the universe has a corresponding appropriate response. Truth remains static and detached until people respond appropriately to it. The appropriate response to the surgeon general's warning would be to stop smoking. Faith requires an exercise of the will; thus, it can be commanded.

The faith of which Jesus spoke in commanding His disciples to believe required the ultimate response. Whereas the response to any truth requires some form of submission, the response to God through Jesus requires complete submission.

### Faith as Trust

The Bible says that Abraham believed God. This belief went beyond believing that God exists. God made a promise to Abraham, and Abraham believed what God told him. Abraham trusted God, and the rest of his life—the rest of human history—was affected by that trust. Of all that God wants from people, it seems the beginning point is trust. If people could only trust God, it would mean the Kingdom had come. Some theologians complain that faith is too simple a basis for salvation. The adoption of a developed system of ethics would give meat and meaning to faith. Someone who has been a Christian for many years, grown in spiritual maturity, and studied the deep matters of the faith may find it easy to believe in a trusting way. Yet in all the world, trust is one of the most difficult spiritual attributes to possess. The rest will come if only that fortress of mistrust can be surrendered. In counseling situations, I have been told over and over again how difficult it is for husbands and wives to trust each other. As a prison chaplain, I have been told by countless men that they have never trusted anyone in their lives. Even as pastor of a church, I have learned that congregations are sometimes suspicious and fearful of what pastors want the church to do. Trust is hard to have. It does not come naturally.

Children are born dependent. They learn trust from their parents and other loving, concerned people. It takes children time to learn that parents can be trusted to feed them, care for them, and not to drop them. Not all children learn to trust. Some parents only prove to their children that no one can be trusted. Some parents prove to their children that the universe is not a safe place. When these children grow up, some of them find themselves facing long prison sentences. It is difficult for them to trust a Heavenly Father they cannot see when the earthly father they could see taught them to hate.

God did not begin by explaining to Abraham the ethical demands of holiness. Instead, He made Abraham a set of promises:

> "Go from your country and your kindred and your father's house to the land that I will show you. And I will make of you a great nation, and I will bless you, and make your name great, so that you will be a blessing. I will bless those who bless you, and him who curses you I will curse; and by you all the families of the earth shall bless themselves" (Gen. 12:1-3).

God did not leave it at that. Instead, He repeated the promise seven times as recorded in Genesis 12:1-3; 13:14-17; 15:1-21; 17:1-21; 18:9-15; 21:12; and 22:16-18.

Abraham trusted the promises of God and did things because of that trust. He left the family, friends, country, language, customs, and religion that he had known because he trusted God. His faith allowed him to make a total break with his past, though he had no basis for action but the word of God. Hebrews expresses it rather poignantly that "he went out, not knowing where he was to go" (Heb. 11:8). Abraham is the model of faith in the Bible because God expects the same sort of response from everyone on earth.

God gave no earth-shaking commission to Abraham. He did not have to preach to anyone and risk stoning like the prophets. He did not have to confront the major world ruler of his time like Moses and lead a nation for forty years. He did not have to be a warrior or a king like David. The only thing God asked Abraham to do was move! The most noteworthy event in his life happened when his wife had a baby! Abraham stands at the center of the Bible as the example of faith. The characteristic of being ordinary makes him an example because the world is filled with ordinary people. Our crises of faith rarely have to do with leading a nation or doing some mighty act. Our crises of faith may center around little ordinary things like moving and having a baby.

Even as I sit writing these words, these two little questions are the greatest ones that probably will face me. Does God want me to stay where I am, or should I move? Does God want me to have a family to rear, or does He want me to devote myself to His family—the church? Trusting God moves from the theoretical to the practical when we begin to make the mundane, commonplace decisions of life. Faith involves living like every decision we face matters to God. Such a faith is grounded in a conviction that God's existence makes a difference in the ordinary events of life as well as the dramatic events of eternity. As an ordinary man, Abraham reminds us that faith is something that affects our lives in the ordinary moments, or it is not faith. Abraham may not have trusted God completely from the first. During a period spanning more than twenty-five years, Abraham's trust in God grew to the point that he could offer his dearest son as a sacrifice to God.

He could never have done that at the beginning when he abandoned the land God had called him to receive and went to Egypt because he feared the famine (Gen. 12:10). He could not have offered Isaac when he lied about his wife for fear that Pharaoh would kill him to get her (Gen. 12:11-13). He could not have offered Isaac when he took Hagar to bed for fear that he would never have a child by Sarah (Gen. 16:2). He could not have offered Isaac when he lied about his wife to Abimelech for fear that someone would kill him to get her (Gen. 20:11). In each of these ordinary passages of life, Abraham's fears were stronger than his trust in God. Yet, after each failure God came to Abraham again with His promises and renewed them over and over.

## Faith and God's Faithfulness

God strengthened Abraham's initial faith by His own faithfulness. Despite the calamities that occurred when Abraham took matters into his own hands, God was faithful to His promise. Abraham believed God in a general, theoretical way, but like most of us, he decided that God needed a little help. Abraham acted as though the promises of God depended upon him and him alone. Each time he took matters into his own hands, he created a mess. He lost his wife twice, and only because of the faithfulness of God did he get her back. Because of his lack of trust, he committed bigamy and created bad blood between brothers that the Arabs and Jews perpetuate to this day. Yet, God remained faithful to His promise and gave Abraham and Sarah the son they wanted.

In the end, Abraham and Sarah had faith in God because God was faithful (Heb. 11:11). Having faith is not the same as being faithful. While having faith involves trust, confidence, and assurance; being faithful involves dependability, reliability, and trustworthiness. In a marriage, it is easy to have faith in a faithful spouse. It is easy to trust a husband or wife who is reliable, dependable, and trustworthy.

Years ago my father brought home a dog. Scout was the most pitiful creature we had ever seen. His black mangy hide exposed every bone in his skinny body. He crouched in fear whenever we approached and bowed his head in anticipation of a blow. The half-starved creature did not trust people. In the first weeks, we had to keep Scout on a chain so he would not run away. As the months passed, however, he learned to trust us. He depended on us to take care of him, and he had confidence that we would. We took the chain off because it was no longer necessary. Scout had learned to trust us for all of his needs, and he chose to stay with us.

Faith is more than a sunny disposition or an optimistic attitude. Faith is more than a vague confidence that things will work out in the end. Unless faith has a basis in life and in God, it is folly. Without a reason for faith, what passes for faith is only wishful thinking. What many Christians attribute to acting by faith may be little more than selfish impulse.

At the same time, faith is not rooted in life's circumstances. Faith occurs in spite of life's circumstances, whether good or bad. Job could say, "Though he slay me, yet will I trust in him" (13:15). His faith did not depend on the changing circumstances of life. Paul said, "I know how to be abased, and I know how to abound; in any and all circumstances I have learned the secret of facing plenty and hunger, abundance and want. I can do all things in him who strengthens me" (Phil. 4:12-13). Faith is rooted in the One who is faithful. The validity and vitality of faith depends upon the object of that faith.

## Faith and Hope

Abraham and Sarah could have hope for a son, even in old age, because of their faith in the One who promised. Hope can be as great a prison as despair if it is not rooted in something or someone worthy of the faith that is trust. Sarah "considered him faithful who had promised" even though Abraham at one hundred years old was "as good as dead" (Heb. 11:11-12). The struggle of faith always hinges on the same principle, regardless of the cold, hard realities of life: "He who promised is faithful" (Heb. 10:23). Thus, God is always the God of the future. He is the God who creates the future.

Faith flies in the face of the kind of cynicism that views life bitterly and fatalistically. *Cynicism* is an attitude of life that has reconciled itself to hopelessness. The prevalence of cynicism finds expression in Murphy's Laws: "Anything that can go wrong will go wrong," "Of all things that could go wrong, the worst of all will go wrong," and "If you mess with anything long enough, it will break." True pagans have no hope because they have nothing in which to place their faith. The cynic knows well the effect of sin in the world. The cynic has experienced the hopelessness of humanity and has accepted it. Hope is an inseparable aspect of faith. Unfortunately, the modern world tends to use the word *hope* the same way it does *wish*. A wish is a fanciful thought or desire that has no basis for being expected. Hope, on the other hand, is a concrete reality, though it is not yet seen. Faith is a form of knowledge which gives assurance of the reality of the hope (Heb. 11:1). Having hope in the midst of a desperate situation goes beyond wishing everything will turn out all right. Having hope means that one has faith that God will act. Abraham's hope was that God would provide him with a son. Hope is a reality which has not yet come to pass, but it is as sure as if it had already happened.

## Faith and Love

Faith also has a dynamic relationship with love, because it is through faith that people permit themselves to be loved by God. God does not impose Himself upon people. We must permit ourselves to be loved. The willingness to be loved or to accept love involves trusting the one who is the lover. God has always loved the world, but people have not always received that love. Through faith, however, "God's love has been poured into our hearts through the Holy Spirit which has been given to us" (Rom. 5:1,5-6). Love in turn becomes the quality of spiritual life that gives direction to faith, preserving it from self-seeking arrogance (Gal. 5:6; 1 Cor. 13:2,5). Love saves faith from becoming a means to an end.

At the end of that last conversation with His disciples, the Lord assured them that the day was coming when they could pray in His name and receive from God: "For the Father himself loves you, because you have loved me and have believed that I came from the Father" (John 16:27). Faith makes true love possible, just as love leads us to have faith in someone. The disciples said that they believed that Jesus came from God. Jesus replied to them with a question: "Do you now believe?" (John 16:31). The irony of the question betrays the events that quickly followed. Human love failed in the absence of true faith. But when true faith in Christ comes, love is made perfect by Him. Jesus brings the change in a human heart when faith opens the door and believes that He really is right.

Faith becomes possible in the first place because of the love of God. God took the initiative to do what was necessary to gain our faith and trust. The sacrifice of Christ on the cross was the ultimate demonstration of faithfulness and trustworthiness: "In this is love, not that we loved God but that he loved us and sent his Son to be the expiation for our sins" (1 John 4:10). Faith grows as a Christian abides in the love of Christ. Abiding in Christ supplies the basis for each dimension of the fruit of a Christian life. Faith continues to grow for the Christian who can say, "I know whom I have believed" (2 Tim. 1:12).

# 10 ||| Meekness

Meekness has an important place among the qualities that describe a life transformed by the Holy Spirit. For the benefit of those concerned with getting ahead in life, Jesus remarked that the meek are a particularly happy lot, because they shall inherit the earth (Matt. 5:5; see Ps. 37:11).

## Meekness Toward Others

Meekness is another one of those spiritual qualities that governs our relationship with other people. Like so many of these qualities, meekness is not something that can be done alone. Persons cannot be meek by themselves; they must have someone else with whom to be meek. Meekness is a way of relating to those both weaker and stronger than we are.

### Toward the Least

Jesus had a lot to say about how to relate to "the least of these." It seems that no matter what our station in life, no matter what our job or income, no matter where we find ourselves, there will always be someone lower on the totem pole than we are. No matter who we are or what age we are, there always seems to be someone with less status and power. Jesus was concerned about how we handle our strength in such a situation.

Jesus looked about Him at the synagogue and the daily life of the time in which He lived; He saw people scrambling to get the most prominent seats in the synagogue. He saw people vying for the most prominent seats at the banquet tables. He saw a generation consumed with the thirst for prestige, status, and social position. In that context, Jesus told a parable about a servant entrusted with the care and administration of a household. No sooner had the master left the house than the servant began to usurp the master's authority. He mistreated the other servants in the household. He only seemed concerned with himself and his own sense of importance. He was charmed by his position of power and eminence. However, having the position was not enough. The servant felt obliged to make the other servants less than what they were (Luke 12:43-46).

I have a friend who used to embarrass me regularly when we went out to eat. Whenever we went to a restaurant, he harassed the waitress. Whatever she did, it was not good enough. She was not quick enough, the food was not hot enough, or he did not have enough tea. He spoke to the waitresses in short, curt comments. He had great power over this "little one." He was not meek with her.

What exactly is *meekness*? The term has a social and economic origin. How often the Bible takes ordinary marketplace words and gives them spiritual significance! Meekness described one who was in the position of a servant in the ancient world. Oddly enough, it is a term Jesus used to describe Himself. He told His disciples to forget their worries, burdens, and way of doing things. He told them to take on His life-style instead, as a yoke, and learn life from Him. And He gave them this reason: "For I am meek and lowly in heart" (Matt. 11:29, KJV).

Jesus wants His disciples to learn meekness from Him. Jesus said that He had come as a servant, not to be served but to serve (Matt. 20:28). This theme was one of the great prophecies of the Old Testament. The prophet Isaiah declared that the Promised One, the Messiah, would come as a Suffering Servant (Isa. 53). That last night, before He was taken, Jesus gathered in the upper room with His disciples and did a strange thing. He took a basin of water and a towel, and He went from disciple to disciple washing their feet. He taught them through the experience that they were to have the attitude of a servant. It would affect how they saw themselves and how they regarded other people. He wanted His disciples to serve people, not lord it over people (Luke 12:42-48).

On Palm Sunday, Jesus entered Jerusalem to the cheers of the crowd acknowledging Him as King. The prophecy that foretold this entry into Jerusalem declared that He would be "meek and riding on an ass" (Matt. 21:5; see Zech. 9:9, KJV). In those days a king or an emperor entered a city to be received as lord. He would enter in a chariot, corresponding to the modern-day tank, a weapon of war. With him would come a full compliment of armed troops, representing power, might, and the ability to rule. The Romans made a great fuss over the show of force one made upon entering a town. The continued respect for the empire depended upon a show of force. But Jesus entered Jerusalem meekly on a small animal. His entry demonstrated what the rule of Christ is like. It is a rule of gentleness with regard to people.

In his spiritual autobiography, Wayne Oates describes an episode in his early life. In front of his house, the street car tracks had a configuration to allow the street cars to bypass each other when they met. The first street car to reach the point would wait for the other one, and they would pass each other at the same time. One street car had a conductor who would laugh and talk with a little boy in that little cotton-mill village. He showed the little boy how the street car operated and answered all the questions that a little boy could think to ask. The great theologian said that he learned from the street car conductor what God is like.

God directs the world. God is powerful, just like the street car conductor who directs a street car. Yet, God is eagerly anxious to take time out for people. He wants to teach people and to laugh with them.

Meekness, however, is more than a smile on the face and a sweet word. It involves more than the superficial cordiality that people put on for social respectability. The formality of social convention can be as devoid of true meekness as overt arrogance.

When Br'er Fox and Br'er B'ar determined to eat Br'er Rabbit for supper, they knew they had to trick Br'er Rabbit because he was too fast and too clever to catch any other way. Br'er Fox knew that despite his small size, Br'er Rabbit did not have an ounce of meekness about him. That is why Br'er Fox reckoned on the plan of making a tar baby, trusting that Br'er Rabbit's lack of meekness would get him stuck.

So, Br'er Fox and Br'er B'ar made a tar baby and put the tar baby on a log beside the road. Br'er Fox put Br'er B'ar's coat and hat on it, Br'er B'ar's pipe in its mouth, and he put the buttons from Br'er B'ar's suspenders for its eyes. Sure enough, it looked like a tar baby. By and by, Br'er Rabbit came down the road. Br'er Rabbit was happy and singing as he hopped along past the tar baby.

"Mornin'," Br'er Rabbit sang out as he hopped along. But lo and behold, he stopped dead in his tracks because the tar baby did not say "mornin' " back to him. So Br'er Rabbit backed up a little bit.

"Mornin'," he sang out and proceeded on his way, knowing that the tar baby would reply. But the tar baby did not say a word. Undone by this turn of events, Br'er Rabbit backed up again.

"How come you don't say mornin' to me when I say mornin' to you?" Br'er Rabbit demanded. But the tar baby did not say a word.

"You see this fist?" Br'er Rabbit said as he made a fist. "If you don't say mornin' to me when I say mornin' to you, I'm gonna put this fist clean through your face. Mornin'!"

But the tar baby did not say a word. Br'er Rabbit was so mad that he slung his fist just as hard as he could into the tar baby's face, and it stuck fast. He got even madder then and proceeded to threaten the tar baby in a terrible way. When the tar baby would not let go of his fist, Br'er Rabbit hit the tar baby with his other fist. And before long, Br'er Rabbit found himself wrapped up in a big ball of tar.

Sometimes the lack of meekness gets people into trouble. When He sent out His disciples, Jesus warned them that they would encounter people who wanted nothing to do with them. He told them not to worry about it but to shake the dust off their feet and go on. He did not want the disciples to become embroiled with false battles like Br'er Rabbit. The haughtiness and arrogance that marked Br'er Rabbit has no place in the life of a Christian because it had no place in the life of Christ.

Br'er Rabbit had such an inflated view of himself that he was absolutely miserable if people did not regard him the way he thought he ought to be regarded. The storybook character was like Cain who grew enraged when God did not regard him highly. In Galatians 6:1, 1 Corinthians 4:21, 2 Corinthians 10:1, and 2 Timothy 2:25, Paul appealed to meekness as the basis for settling disputes between Christians—because Jesus was meek.

### Toward Those in Authority

Though meekness is required of Christians in dealing with those weaker than they, it is also required in dealing with those who are stronger. Meekness is required in dealing with those whom the Bible calls the authorities. Christians are subject to the authorities (Rom.

13:1). In the face of authority, Christians face the problem of handling their weaknesses in the presence of another's strength.

Often people will relate to authority rebelliously. I have a friend who once taught mathematics in a small private school in a small Southern town made up largely of extremely wealthy families from the North. The rich immigrants came South largely because of the horse community which indulged in polo and riding to the hounds. They thrived on breeding and racing horses. Among the children in that private school were representatives of some of the wealthiest families in the country.

My friend encountered an incredible rebelliousness on the part of the children in his classroom. They enforced their rebelliousness by reminding my friend, "My father pays your salary, and I don't have to do what you say." When I was a child, we used the expression *stuck up* to describe the arrogant, haughty, and conceited attitudes that marked these children. Oddly enough, this attitude is not even based on who we are as individuals, but it is based on the merit of someone else. The children attempted to exert a power and authority they did not have, though they deluded themselves into believing they had it. In their conceit, they exempted themselves from the authority of their teacher.

The same sort of thing happened with the people who refused to listen to Jesus because they were the children of Abraham. They did not believe they needed to be taught by Jesus, and they refused to submit to His authority (John 8:31-59). This rebelliousness which refuses instruction is the very opposite of meekness.

Meekness involves teachability. In the Book of James the relationship between meekness and teachability is drawn out: "Therefore, put away all filthiness and rank growth of wickedness and receive with meekness the implanted word, which is able to save your souls" (Jas. 1:21). Meekness makes learning a possibility.

The meekness of Jesus grew out of His relationship to the Father. In relation to the strength of His Father, Jesus acknowledged His own weakness. Jesus said, "I can do nothing on my own authority" (John 5:30; see 8:28). His meekness allowed Him to grow in wisdom (Luke 2:52).

## Meekness as an Attitude Toward Self

If meekness involves how people relate to one another, it begins with a person's attitude toward himself or herself. Meekness requires self-acceptance. Meekness grows out of a sure acceptance of who we are. Self-esteem does not depend on exercising control over others or rebelling against the authority of others. Our worth and value as individuals stands independently of how others view our importance.

### Self-Acceptance Verses Arrogance

Arrogance, on the other hand, is self-rejection. We are not satisfied with who we are. We wish we were someone else, and we wish everyone saw us as someone else. Arrogant persons need constant acknowledgment that they are important. They constantly need to prove how important and powerful they are.

Revenge is a constant theme in the subculture of the mafia. Gang wars and vendettas form the backdrop of organized crime. Respect is enforced by violence and retribution, and honor depends upon one's ability to enforce respect. In a gang war or vendetta, a gangster does not make peace for fear that it will appear as weakness.

Arrogance tends to be governed totally by the question: "What will people think of me?" This preoccupation, in a sense, gives everyone else the power to govern the arrogant person who cannot accept who he or she is. Arrogant people become stage performers who require applause, or its equivalent, from the crowd.

Such a man was Haman, grand vizier to Ahasuerus. Haman's self-esteem came from the external demonstrations of power, such as the mandatory bowing of all subordinates. Though having people bow and scrape brought a surge of exhilaration to his ego, it was only an artificial high that did not affect Haman's heart in a positive way. Quite the contrary. It was such a poor substitute for true self-esteem and self-worth that it made him feel all the worse when a single individual failed to bow to him. Haman's ruin, as recorded in the Book of Esther, stemmed from his obsession with forcing recognition from others. Haman required the artificial show of recognition because he lacked the self-assurance of those at peace with who they are. When Mordecai would not bow to Haman, none of the others who bowed could supply him with what Mordecai took away.

Arrogance drives at creating artificial props for the frail human spirit. Arrogance also supplies the creative force necessary to invent status symbols. The intellect might be clever enough to notice the foolishness of status symbols if it were not for the overwhelming emotional power of arrogance to short-circuit the mental process. Those consumed with the need to be recognized cannot exhibit meekness. Their spirits are too preoccupied with wresting admiration, adulation, and appreciation from others to ever take on the form of a servant.

Even arrogance, however, can be expressed in the costume of humility. The charade of meekness is as good a way as any of drawing attention to oneself as being worthy of the esteem of others. In *David Copperfield*, Charles Dickens created the figure of Uriah Heap, a particularly despicable character who embezzled the wealth of his clients. Heap pathetically described himself as a very humble person as he deferred to others of wealth and breeding. In fact, Heap despised those to whom he deferred as he plotted his rise at the expense of their ruin. Heap reasoned that he would be as good as everyone else if he had money, then he could look down on other people.

The history of the human race is filled with people who have sought power, wealth, sex, or any of innumerable means human creativity has devised for creating the illusion of worth. The desperation of this pursuit indicates the enormity of the sense of worthlessness which most people feel. Arrogance, pride, and vanity are only emotional props to cover the emptiness. They are the fuel that generates a consumer economy in which clothing styles and automobile designs change every year. They are the reason for an advertising philosophy that makes a sensual appeal rather than an intellectual appeal. The absence of arrogance, however, does not mean the presence of meekness. Many people have come to grips with the vanity of vanities only to face the reality of their own sense of worthlessness. Without the narcotic luxury of arrogance and pride, one must live with one's own sense of inadequacy and insignificance. These are the people who thrive on self-pity. Meekness cannot be imposed, however, by life's circumstances. A meek person is never a victim of life's unfairness. Meekness is a choice made from strength, not weakness.

*Self-Acceptance Verses Self-Pity*

Self-pity may dress in the guise of meekness, but like arrogance, it constantly cries for attention. Self-pity leads individuals to believe that no one cares for them. They do not care for themselves, so why should anyone else? Self-pitying people accept the same values as arrogant people, but find that they cannot secure the props of status. Lacking what they believe confers worth and value, self-pitying people judge themselves to be worthless.

In the United States, sports has become the national religion and cult of a competitive, strength-oriented culture. Beauty of body and extraordinary physical performance are the focal points of worship. The handicapped, the maimed, the disfigured, or the inadequate simply suffer the judgment of worthlessness to the values of the culture. Those who accept this valuation sink into self-pity. To the same extent, those who lack the financial resources to compete in fashion, housing, and luxuries stand labeled by the community. What is worse is, when they accept the community's valuation, they fall into self-condemnation!

While Haman used power and intrigue to force recognition and attention from others, the self-pitying person uses the practiced manipulative skills of self-deprecation. The talented choir member with low self-esteem can always wrench a compliment from friends by saying, "I didn't sing very well today."

A protest will follow. As though someone held a gun to their heads, the friends will fall in line and say, "Oh, you sang beautifully." Oddly enough, when the tactic has succeeded in forcing attention from others, the poor soul feels no better.

The self-pitying person can no more express meekness than the arrogant person. Self-pity is an attitude of total preoccupation with oneself. The preoccupation revolves around what persons lack that they believe would make their lives complete—if only they had it. Self-pity is fueled by a passionate desire for the missing ingredient, and it is often accompanied by envy and jealousy of those who have the missing ingredient. The self-pitying person's misery comes from having accepted the values of the world rather than the worth of Christ. Both arrogance and self-pity betray a pathetic self-rejection.

## Self-Acceptance Based on Christ

Meekness on the other hand requires a self-acceptance that does not demand constant attention and reassurance of one's importance. Meekness is the outer badge of the calm assurance that the Spirit of Christ brings. By our abiding in Christ, His Holy Spirit frees us from the desire to prove ourselves or in some way make ourselves great. He brings the satisfaction that comes with being a child of God, being made in the image of Christ. In Christ, we realize that we are a special treasure of immense value to God. So precious and valuable are we that God entered the world of pain and sorrow through His only begotten Son, bore the misery and guilt of sin on the cross, and delivered us from the rule of sin. We are worth enough for Christ to die for us. Meekness becomes a possibility when we have assurance and confidence in our relationship to the Lord.

Freed from an overwhelming preoccupation with our own standing or lack of standing, a Christian can follow the example of the Lord, who in meekness took on the form of a servant. The vain standards of recognition and importance fade in the presence of the Lord. The yearning to have attention dissolves in the love of God as the Christian abides in Christ.

# 11 ||| Self-Control

Sometimes people notice how out of control they really are, but not very often. On these rare occasions, people notice how little control they have over what they are doing. This lack of control is easiest to notice in relation to our bodies.

## Out of Control

Sometimes my body seems attracted to the refrigerator. I have marveled at how many trips I can make to the refrigerator to get something to drink in the course of an afternoon. Other people will make just as many trips to get something to eat. They get nothing much, just something. The compulsion to eat takes control. At such times, we lose control of our bodies. Chain smokers know the meaning of being out of control of their bodies. Alcoholics live with the same lack of control as though they must obey the commands of some other voice. Money can affect other people the same way. Those who feel compelled to spend money feel the same inability to control themselves that the chain smoker experiences.

The opposite situation holds the same lack of control. Some people have such a compulsion not to eat that they literally starve themselves to death. Karen Carpenter, a famous singer of the 1970s, suffered from the inability to control her own body's needs and desires.

Though all of these expressions of being out of control have a physical dimension, they are governed by spiritual motivations. Emotions can control people just as physical addictions or habits can. When people lose control of their emotions, they become as enslaved as a person who is physically addicted to a substance. Feelings of anger, fear, depression, or inferiority may become characteristic of a person just as wine is for the wino.

When people lose control of their feelings, they become as addicted toand controlled by their feelings as someone whose life is controlled by drugs or sex. They depend upon their habitual emotional fix to cope with life and get through the day. They become comfortable with and learn to rely upon the emotions that control them.

The subtlety of this emotional slavery makes it easy to ignore and deny. The alcoholic who denies that drinking is a problem has the benefit of alcohol's physical nature to help him see the problem. (It must be purchased, poured, and drunk; it has an effect on the body; and alcohol's effect can be observed.) The spiritual nature of an emotional slavery, however, lacks the external physical agent that can be both recognized and blamed. To recognize an emotional addiction, one must confess guilt.

Among the works of the flesh, we find more than drunkenness, fornication, and murder. The works of the flesh also include envy, jealousy, selfishness, enmity, strife, dissension, and factionalism (Gal. 5:19-21). People can become just as—if not more—addicted to these emotions and attitudes as other people become addicted to physical stimulants. People can be just as hooked on jealousy as on alcohol.

When we become addicted to a habitual form of behavior or to a physical craving, we tend to surrender passively to the force of it. We simply give up and let it have control of us. Self-control, the last quality in Paul's list that manifests the Spirit of God in the life of a Christian, deals directly with this problem.

## Getting a Hold

The Greek word *self-control* is a compound word. Literally, *egkrateia* might be translated inward power or power and strength to hold on. It draws the visual image of persons wrapping their arms around themselves and holding themselves. It is reflected in the modern phrase, "Get a hold of yourself." The word itself tells us that we are not powerless or helpless. We can do something about these compulsions in our lives. It also tells us that we are responsible for ourselves.

One would think that such an important word would be found over and over again in the New Testament, but it only occurs a few times. There is a good reason for its rarity, however. It might be confused with an idea in Greek philosophy. Christians living in the Hellenistic world, such as Ephesus, Galatia, Corinth, and Rome, might have confused the Christian concept of self-control with a Greek philosophical

idea—definitely not Christian—linked to the same word. Unfortunately, that philosophical idea has found its way into Christianity, and
many people have accepted it through the years as orthodox.

The Greeks developed one school of thought that advocated self-
denial, but not in the Christian sense. They believed in the avoidance
and denial of the physical world. They believed they would attain immortality by personally overcoming the world. They viewed the material world as evil and not the result of creation by a loving God. Physical reality was a mistake or worse. A state of perfection, however,
could be reached by strict discipline and asceticism.

In the modern world, this self-centered approach to one's place in
life might be expressed, "I am the master of my fate; I am the captain
of my soul."[1] Hemingway subscribed to this type of philosophy,
though not in its ascetic form. In Hemingway, this philosophy of self-
control came in his choice to die. When faced with cancer, Hemingway decided that he would choose the moment of his death, and he
committed suicide.

The emphasis in the New Testament on the concept of self-control
is quite different. It emphasizes the unnaturalness of self-control. People do not naturally have self-control. It comes as a gift from God.
Instead of my being the captain of my ship, "the master of my fate,"
and the ruler of my life, I am a steward. I am a servant who has been
entrusted with this life. Self-control is an aspect of my stewardship
responsibility to God. Though God has given me life or made me
alive, I am still His possession.

Jesus told a parable about a lord who went on a journey into a
distant country. Before going, the master left his servants in care of
certain goods. God has given me the care of my life, but to take of it
He has given me gifts and abilities and has equipped us to carry out
the task. A passage in 2 Timothy tells how self-control comes to people: "God did not give us a spirit of timidity but a spirit of power and
love and self-control" (1:7). God gives self-control as a possibility
when His Holy Spirit comes to abide in the heart of a believer.

Unlike Hemingway, the apostle Paul faced death with the Christian
view of self-control. Paul's death lay within the control of his captors,
but he had control within himself. He expressed that sense of control
with the words, "I can do all things through Christ which strengthen-
eth me" (Phil. 4:13, KJV). Paul knew that he had the ability through

Christ to stand up to, face, and deal with whatever happened in life. That knowledge, personal knowledge of Christ and confidence in Him, gave Paul full control of his life. Self-control freed him from fear or depression or any other enslaving compulsion which might have threatened the experience of that other quality of the Spirit's presence: joy.

Self-control in itself is not a human characteristic. Rather, it is a divine gift, alien to the human nature. It involves more than merely abstaining from something. It involves more than trying to conquer a habit, compulsion, or addiction. People can do that to a certain extent. Breaking habits and fighting compulsions can be frustrating because the human effort at control only deals with the negative dimension of trying to stop. In trying to stop, people dwell on the very thing they are trying to avoid. The battle makes the obstacle even more present in the mind.

Producing fruit involves pruning out the bad, but it also involves fertilizing. Something positive and life giving must be added for fruit to appear. Abstaining is only one dimension, and it is the negative dimension. But what about the more important life-giving dimension?

## Gaining a Balance

In the old authorized translation of the Bible, commonly known as the *King James Version*, the translators chose to render this word as temperance. They retained the word from the Vulgate, the old Latin Bible used by the Roman Catholic Church, which dated back to the fifth century. *Temperance* comes from the Latin word *temperare* which means to mix in due proportions. In applying this idea to life, it becomes a matter of having an appropriate balance and mixture in life. Temperance involves the appropriate mixture and balance of all the elements of life.

Temperance or self-control depends upon having this balance. It involves having a balanced temper. To lay the charge that someone has a temper confuses the point we mean to make. The explosiveness usually associated with *having a temper* rarely occurs when someone truly has a balanced temper. Instead of saying, "John has a temper," we ought to say, "John has a bad temper." This expression captures the faultiness of one's ability to maintain a temper or balance. A corruptible temper may not be relied upon to maintain control of the delicate interactions of one's emotions in a crisis. We might also say, "John has lost his temper." When we lose our tempers or our balance, we have lost our ability to control ourselves. We have let go the mechanism by which we exercise sovereignty over ourselves and become like a machine without a driver. When someone tells us to keep our tempers or hold our tempers, what are they saying? They are urging us to hold on to our balance, not to fly off on a tangent, and to control ourselves.

To temper something involves reducing its intensity by the addition of something else. When we make iced tea, we put three bags in a small tea pot and let the tea steep. But the brew is too intense to drink like it is. It has to be diluted or tempered by the addition of cold water. Even though we set out to make tea, when it becomes too intense it ceases to be good. The tea becomes overpowering when the balance with water is not right. Just like the tea, the emotions that play a part in our health and happiness can become bitter and overpowering when one grows out of balance with the rest.

A person with a good sense of humor is a pleasant person to be around. He or she brings joy to a conversation. On the other hand, a person who constantly tells jokes, monopolizing the conversation and attention of others, is a tiresome bore. We normally avoid bores. They have no temper or balance to their conversations. Whether the practical jokers, the workaholics who can only talk about jobs, the hypochondriacs who can only talk about poor health, or the socialites who can only talk about connections, those who allow one small passion to dominate their lives have lost control of themselves. They are out of balance and have no temper.

The first computer game I played involved maintaining the right balance in resources. The game involved a hypothetical trip across the continent by covered wagon in pioneer days. The player was allowed a ration of supplies, animals, and money at the outset. In the course of the game, the player was beset by Indians, snowstorms, and other disasters which depleted the resources for the trip. The only way to win the game was to maintain the proper balance of resources so that none ran out before the journey was complete.

Like the hypothetical pioneer in the game, people must bring together a variety of resources to temper the excesses in their lives. An alloy has strength that its constituent metals lack individually. Self-control involves bringing together resources which create strength in proper balance. How we view ourselves determines what qualities we can bring to bear to temper the excesses of our lives. When people focus their lives and energy on just one dimension of life, regardless of how good that dimension might be in proper balance, they have lost control. They have a false idea of just how varied and strong their potential resources are. People who focus on a sense of inferiority and failure become too consumed by that passion to notice just how many resources they actually have to keep them balanced and give them control. An old folk proverb testifies to this truth: all work and no play makes Jack a dull boy. Focusing on just one dimension of life takes away the possibility of self-control.

Self-control or temperance involves balancing the budget of human resources and activity. Failure to have this balance breeds disaster. Anyone who has tried to run a home knows that one must keep one's income and expenditures properly balanced, or personal financial disaster will follow. The homemaker soon learns to exercise control in what and how much one buys. Some expenditures must be put off for a long time. Corporations that fail to maintain the right balance in cash flow and inventory go bankrupt. People become personally bankrupt when they fail to maintain a balance of their emotions, passions, and desires.

Without self-control, we become the slaves of what we focus on. Persons can become slaves of gossip just as easily as to drugs. Persons can become addicted to feeling sorry for themselves just as they may become enslaved to sexual perversion. Such slavery destroys our opportunities and potential for free living. When our lives become focused on one object, that object becomes our ruling passion.

Paul almost frantically warned the Galatians about this form of slavery, for "those who belong to Christ Jesus have crucified the flesh with its passions and desires" (5:24). The works of the flesh which Paul enumerated do not constitute an exhaustive list. Rather they indicate the variety of passions and desires that can control and bind us. Things—whether they be objects, ideas, or people—to which we give up our freedom and responsibility are the works of the flesh. Paul pointed out a small category of areas in which the work of the flesh can be seen, but he added that the works of the flesh include not simply these things listed in Galatians 5:19-21 but also "the like." Works of the flesh which prevent people from inheriting the kingdom of God include anything like these compulsions to which people give up the control of their lives. Any passion which people allow to dominate them is a work of the flesh. Any desire which people allow to control them until it becomes a ruling passion in thought and action, so that they no longer feel they have freedom of action, constitutes a work of the flesh. Whenever people feel moved by compulsion, addiction, or habit they have lost control.

The essence of the demonic is to be possessed and out of control of oneself. The tragedy of such possession lies in the human invitation and surrender to the passion that becomes the master. The entire soul becomes the slave of a desire.

## Confessing What Controls Us as Sin

How can we deal with the passions and desires that control us? First of all, we must name the passion that controls us. Freedom begins in knowing our weakness and susceptibility. Not everyone has the same weakness. Not everyone is subject to the same passions and desires. Some people are subject to physical addictions while others have emotional addictions. The desires of some will offer no allure to others. Even the physical addictions, however, have some ultimate emotional/spiritual origin. While some people may fall unknowingly into a physical addiction, most people are aware of the potential danger, but they are driven on by some passion within them before they have ever tasted what will eventually be their master.

Alcoholism has had a prominent career in my family. It was a curse to the Poes long before Edgar Allen. I might have become an alcoholic, if I had begun to drink recreationally. In the southern genteel society in which I was reared, it was expected of men to drink. A socially prominent woman once explained to a group of my friends as teenagers that it might be possible for a woman to survive in society without drinking, but it was impossible for a man. The passion and desire to conform to the expectations of others has led many people into physical addictions of one kind or another. Any number of other emotional tyrants could bring about the same result. In reclaiming self-control, naming the original passion is as important for the physically addicted person as recognizing that one has a physical addiction.

When I became a Baptist minister, I removed myself from polite society by virtue of my new status. Polite society has never known exactly what to do with ministers. Since polite society no longer claimed me as one of its own, it no longer insisted that I drink, and I have never had the inclination to begin. I do not know the struggles of the alcoholic, but I have other passions which are just as destructive to my soul.

Not long ago, I had lunch with a pastor friend. Another pastor friend of ours had recently been called to serve as pastor of an enormous church, and my friend asked how I thought the other would do in his new position. In a flash, my heart filled with envy and jealousy as I thought of our friend in his prominent and wealthy church. I had to confess to my friend those feelings that went through me. Once I had recognized my feelings and confessed them to someone else, their power waned to a barely perceptible memory. Then in reflection as we talked about it, I knew just how ridiculous my passion had been. The last thing I wanted at that point in my life was a large church to administer. The church my friend went to, though prominent and wealthy, is riddled with problems and caused the last pastor no end of headaches. Despite my passion, the reality was that I did not want to be in a situation like my friend. The great deceit of the works of the flesh is that they are not really what we want.

The works of the flesh are substitutes for what people really want and need. Lust is a substitute for love. Sorcery and idolatry are substitutes for a personal relationship with God. When we name and confess the thing that is controlling us, however, we begin to have an upper hand. Self-control does not emerge from our strengths. On the contrary, it grows out of our weaknesses. In confession we face and acknowledge our weaknesses while calling on God for help. When we realize we cannot do anything about the passion and cry out for help, the focus of our attention suddenly turns from the problem to God, the Giver of help.

Paul says, "If we live by the Spirit, let us also walk by the Spirit" (Gal. 5:25). We are not saved by our own efforts, and we are not sanctified by our own efforts. Both are brought about by the Holy Spirit. In developing those spiritual qualities that the Spirit makes possible, Christians have something to mix with their lives and give balance to the urges that obsess them. Battling the demon keeps us tied to the passion. Worrying about the demon keeps us tied to the passion.

Dwelling on the demon keeps us tied to the passion. When Christians focus on the qualities that describe what a Spirit-led life is like, they drown out the passions of the flesh. Life becomes tempered by the fruit of the Spirit in a Christian's life. Self-control brings other good qualities to bear on a Christian's life.

These qualities that Paul has enumerated to describe the fruit of the Spirit are part of the transforming consequence of the presence of the Holy Spirit in a person's life. In each case, God is the Model for these qualities. Self-control models or reflects the marvelous perfection of God by which all of His attributes are perfectly balanced. God mingles His wrath with love. He mingles His justice with mercy. When God has mingled all of His qualities together in perfect proportion, He is not a God to hold in terror. He is a God of perfection to whom we are drawn.

It is His Spirit that dwells in us when we have faith in the atoning death and resurrection of Jesus Christ. He urges us to walk in His Spirit in order that His character will begin to appear in our lives. The Spirit will transform a person until their character conforms to the image of the Spirit Himself. The only inhibiting factor is the person's refusal to be transformed. When a person is willing to be transformed, the transformation takes place until the human spirit corresponds to the character of the Holy Spirit. It occurs as a result of the new nature.

## Notes

1. William Ernest Henley, "Invictus," *Masterpieces of Religious Verse,* ed. James Dalton Morrison (Nashville: Broadman Press, 1977), 575-76.

# 12 ||| The New Covenant

After describing the fruit of the Spirit, Paul observed that "against such there is no law" (Gal. 5:23). The law had come as a result of God's covenant with Israel when He brought them out of Egypt. As such, the law served as the standard of behavior for the nation. It revealed the righteous will of God, yet it did not make people righteous. Instead, it supplied a basis for determining when people had sinned and how they should be punished. The law condemned many to death, but it did not grant life to anyone.

While the law of Moses might control behavior through threat of punishment, it could not produce love, joy, peace, and the other character traits of God in the people. The law could only do so much, and it does not stand against what goes beyond it. The freedom of the Spirit, on the other hand, does not invalidate the truth of the law. The covenant of the law simply served to prepare the world for a new and more glorious covenant (Gal. 3:24).

Earlier in the Book of Galatians, Paul had posed the question, "Is the law then against the promises of God?" (3:21). The transformation of people which the law could not produce came as the result of promises God had made through the prophets. The transformation that could not come through obedience to the law now comes through faith in Jesus Christ. While the covenant of the law provided a basis for relationship with God, it did not provide a means of justification and transformation. To achieve this end, God gave the promise of a new covenant to His people.

Apart from the new covenant, one strives in vain to produce the fruit of the Spirit. Apart from the new covenant, people could not become like Christ. God delivered the promise clearly through Jeremiah who foretold:

"Behold, the days are coming, says the Lord, when I will make a new covenant with the house of Israel and the house of Judah, not like the covenant which I made with their fathers when I took them by the hand to bring them out of the land of Egypt, my covenant which they broke, though I was their husband, says the Lord. But this is the covenant which I will make with the house of Israel after those days, says the Lord: I will put my law within them, and I will write it upon their hearts; and I will be their God, and they shall be my people. And no longer shall each man teach his neighbor and each his brother, saying, 'Know the Lord,' for they shall all know me, from the least of them to the greatest, says the Lord; for I will forgive their iniquity, and I will remember their sin no more" (Jer. 31:31-34).

The prophet Ezekiel brought the word that God would "put a new spirit within" His people (Ezek. 11:19). While the old covenant served to expose sin, the new covenant would serve to forgive sin and change the sinful heart.

## The Lord's Supper

Throughout this examination of the fruit of the Spirit, we have referred to the Last Supper when Jesus spoke of many of these qualities to His disciples. Before saying anything about the quality of life they could expect through abiding in Him, however, He declared to them the new covenant. For centuries, the Jewish people had celebrated the Passover. They had taken the unleaven bread and the cup from generation to generation as they told their children the story of how God redeemed Israel from bondage. On that night, however, Jesus interrupted a thousand years or more of tradition. This time, the meal meant more than it ever had meant before.

In his Gospel, Luke recorded what happened as they observed the Passover:

He took bread, and when he had given thanks he broke it and gave it to them, saying, "This is my body which is given for you. Do this in remembrance of me." And likewise the cup after supper, saying, "This cup which is poured out for you is the old covenant in my blood" (Luke 22:19-20).

In Matthew's account of the event, he includes that the blood "is poured out for many for the forgiveness of sins" (Matt. 26:28).

Jesus gave new meaning to the meal. He came to bring the new covenant. The Passover meal which had symbolized the old covenant of Israel now formed a bridge for understanding the new covenant. Instead of discarding the Passover meal as no longer significant, the followers of Jesus clung to the meal as a symbolic explanation of what Christ had done. When He said, "Do this in remembrance of me," He did not mean in a sentimental way not to forget Him when He was gone. He meant for us to observe the meal in order to keep fresh the meaning of the new covenant. He meant for us to remember constantly the magnitude of the salvation that came as a result of the new covenant.

## Freedom from Death

The Passover meal recalled the events surrounding the Exodus from Egypt. The name recalled the final crisis which prompted Pharaoh to release the enslaved children of Israel. Nine times God had sent plagues upon Egypt, and nine times Pharaoh had resisted the command to let Israel go. Finally, God announced the final plague. He would pass through the land of Egypt and slay the firstborn child in every house from the palace of Pharaoh to the hut of the lowliest Egyptian slave. In issuing the threat, however, God provided a way of escape. If anyone would slay a lamb and place its blood on the lintel and door posts of the house, then God would "pass over" that house and no harm would come (Ex. 12:23).

God was not allergic to the lamb's blood. It contained no magic power, nor did it in anyway serve to appease God. It demonstrated that people believed what God said and trusted Him to save them. All those who believed God acted on their faith, and death passed over their homes. A parallel experience occurred during the wilderness wandering when Israel sinned against God. God caused serpents to bite the people, which resulted in sickness and death. Again, however, God provided a way of escape. He instructed Moses to fashion a bronze serpent and set it on a pole in the middle of the camp. Anyone who looked at the bronze serpent would live. Once again, the serpent had no magical power. In fact, King Hezekiah destroyed the serpent years later when the people of Judah began to worship it as magical (2 Kings 18:4). God healed the people because they acted on their faith. They believed what He said. Jesus used the example of the serpent to illustrate how faith operates in salvation: "As Moses lifted up the serpent in the wilderness, so must the Son of man be lifted up, that who-ever believes in him may have eternal life" (John 3:14-15). Both the plague of death of the firstborn and the episode of the serpents in the wilderness demonstrate the gravity of the human situation. The hovering nearness of calamity reinforces the need for a Savior.

In the Passover meal, the Jewish people recall how death passed over them in a historical situation at one time and place long ago. In the Lord's Supper, however, Christ promises that death will pass over not just temporarily but for all time for all who look to Him in faith. The blood of Christ replaces the blood of the paschal lamb placed on the lintels and door posts. Paul referred to Christ as our paschal lamb (1 Cor. 15:1-7). In his Gospel, John described the crucifixion as coinciding with the prescribed time for the "Preparation of the Passover" (John 19:14). As Jesus went to His death, the priests began killing the Passover lambs.

## Freedom from Sin

In the Exodus, God not only saved some from death, but He also saved the nation from bondage to Pharaoh. In the Lord's Supper, Christ promises freedom from the bondage of sin as well as the bondage of death. The Passover celebrated liberation for people held as slaves. Paul spoke of Christians in the same terms in Galatians a few verses before describing the fruit of the Spirit. He declared: "For freedom Christ has set us free; stand fast therefore, and do not submit again to a yoke of slavery" (Gal. 5:1). The Passover recalls that God freed a particular people in a particular place and time from a particular slavery. In the Lord's Supper, Christ offers to free people in all places and times from the slavery of sin and death if they will have faith in Him.

While the Exodus changed the physical condition of Israel, it did not change the spiritual condition of the people. They left Egypt free from the yoke of slavery, but the ensuing events in their journey to the Promised Land indicate that they remained enslaved to sin. The covenant of the law did not release them from that bondage. The law did not make them holy, nor did it justify them before God. In fact, the law increased the guilt of sin because it abolished the excuse of ignorance: "What then shall we say? That the law is sin? By no means! Yet, if it had not been for the law, I should not have known sin. I should not have known what it is to covet if the law had not said, 'You shall not covet' " (Rom. 7:7). But under the new covenant, salvation means freedom from the reign of sin, "For sin will have no dominion over you, since you are not under law but under grace" (Rom. 6:14).

## Freedom from the Law

God gave the law as holy and righteous (Rom. 3:21; 7:12). Because of the sinful nature of the human race, however, it served to accuse rather than excuse. With pathos, the Scripture explains: "For all who rely on works of the law are under a curse; for it is written, 'Cursed be every one who does not abide by all things written in the book of the law, and do them' " (Gal. 3:10). By giving knowledge of sin and making people accountable for their sins, the law served as an overwhelming burden. As long as the covenant of the law stood in effect, it kept people bound to the curse of their own sin.

When Christ came, however, He fulfilled the law in all its demands and thus accomplished its purpose. Once fulfilled, it could be replaced by a superior covenant. Jesus Himself explained that He had not "come to abolish the law and the prophets;" instead, He came "to fulfil them" (Matt. 5:17). Jesus did not appear suddenly on the stage of history and announce that He intended to start a new religion. He came as the climax of the religion of Israel. He constantly reminded His followers that He stood in continuity with the faith of Israel, not as a rival to it. The New Testament frequently refers to Christ's coming as a fulfillment, and Jesus insisted that He came in accordance with the promises of God (Luke 24:27; Acts 2:22-36; 7:2-53; and 13:17-41).

The new covenant frees those who have faith in Christ from the legal demands and penalties of the law. Christ accomplished this liberation on the cross: "having canceled the bond which stood against us with its legal demands; this he set aside, nailing it to the cross" (Col. 2:14). Thus, Christ not only frees from sin and death under the new covenant but also from the just penalties of the old covenant. The Lord's Supper symbolizes not only the freedom Christ brings, but also the manner in which He brought the freedom. A substitution took place: "Christ redeemed us from the curse of the law, having become a curse for us . . . that we might receive the promise of the Spirit through faith" (Gal. 3:13-14). Through His death, Christ fulfilled the letter of the law by substituting Himself for the guilty parties. Settling the requirements of the law once and for all, He opened the way for the new covenant.

Christ ended the curse of the law by assuming the curse. Salvation came through the plan and initiative of God. Only by direct intervention of God could the continual cause/effect law of sin and death be broken:

> For the law of the Spirit of life in Christ Jesus has set me free from the law of sin and death. For God has done what the law, weakened by the flesh, could not do: sending his own Son in the likeness of sinful flesh and for sin, he condemned sin in the flesh, in order that the just requirement of the law might be fulfilled in us, who walk not according to the flesh but according to the Spirit (Rom. 8:2-4).

Jesus reflected this mission to fulfill the law when He came to John for baptism. John balked, realizing his own unworthiness to baptize Jesus, but Jesus replied, "Let it be so now; for thus it is fitting for us to fulfill all righteousness" (Matt. 3:15).

## Redemption

By virtue of His death, Christ became the Redeemer. In the Old Testament, the redeemer served as a mediator or stood in on behalf of the next of kin. The redeemer vindicated, avenged, or fulfilled the obligations of kinsmen powerless to help themselves. Boaz obtained the right of redemption in the case of the estate of Elimelech. As redeemer, Boaz had the first right to purchase the property to keep it in the family, but he also incurred the obligation to marry Ruth so that the dead husband would have an heir (Ruth 4:1-10). Job longed for a Redeemer to stand between him and God to justify him (Job 19:25). In the case of the Passover, it recalled when God declared Himself the Redeemer of Israel. Since Israel could not free herself from bondage, God came as a stand in, as the next of kin: "Say therefore to the people of Israel, I am the Lord, and I will bring you out from under the burdens of the Egyptians, and I will deliver you from their bondage, and I will redeem you with an outstretched arm and with great acts of judgment' " (Ex. 6:6). As Redeemer, God fought against Pharaoh as the substitute for Israel, too weak to fight her own battle.

As Redeemer of the world, Christ stood in our place with respect to the law, sin, and death. As Redeemer, He fulfilled all obligations to the law with respect to sin and death. The law had not brought death. Sin had brought death, but the law brought the knowledge of the relationship between sin and death. As Redeemer, Jesus took upon Himself the sin and death of the ones He loved as next of kin: "Therefore he is the mediator of a new covenant, so that those who are called may receive the promised eternal inheritance, since a death has occurred which redeems them from the transgressions under the first covenant" (Heb. 9:15). Hebrews stresses that Christ came into the world "so that by the grace of God he might taste death for every one" (Heb. 2:9). As Redeemer, Christ died as a substitute.

The idea of the substitute permeated the old covenant. The yearly observance of the Passover taught the concept. When the Lord commanded Moses and the Israelites to keep the Passover every year, He commanded that they should set apart all the firstborn for a sacrifice to God as a memorial. The commandment extended to all animals and people! With the commandment, however, came the provision for redemption. Though the firstborn children stood consigned to death as a sacrifice of thanksgiving, God also ordered that they be redeemed: "All the firstlings of your cattle that are males shall be the Lord's. Every firstling of an ass you shall redeem with a lamb, or if you will not redeem it you shall break its neck. Every first-born of man among your sons you shall redeem" (Ex. 13:12-13). While the old covenant served to condemn, it also had contained within it from its inception the means of deliverance by redemption. By implication, this concept suggested that a redeemer could take the place of those who stood accused under the law because of sin.

### Forgiveness

The old covenant never offered forgiveness of sin in a complete and finished fashion. The old covenant provided for sin offerings, and the most solemn observance of Israel came on the annual Day of Atonement when the High Priest made sacrifice to God for the sins of Israel and himself (Lev. 16). Under the old covenant, sacrificial laws provided for an appropriate offering for every sin a person might commit. Every sin required an offering, and the fire of the altar remained kindled by the priests to carry out the unending ritual of sacrifice for the people who brought their offerings.

Because of the continual problem of sin, the people had the continuing necessity to seek forgiveness through the means provided under the law. The law itself demonstrated the inability of people to solve the problem of their own sin and the separation it caused between them and God. In the new covenant, however, Christ brought to an end the need for the perpetual offering of sacrifice:

> But when Christ had offered for all time a single sacrifice for sins, he sat down at the right hand of God, then to wait until his enemies should be made a stool for his feet. For by a single offering he has perfected for all time those who are sanctified. . . . Where there is forgiveness of these, there is no longer any offering for sin (Heb. 10:12-14,18).

The death of Christ satisfied the demand of the law for a sacrifice. Religions all over the world have practiced continual sacrifice, but God put an end to sacrifices through Christ who offered Himself as a final sacrifice (Heb. 9:26). Unlike the goats and bulls sacrificed on the altars without their consent, Christ offered Himself—giving a profoundly ethical dimension to the new covenant.

More than satisfying the legal demand of the law with respect to sin, however, the death of Christ brought forgiveness of sin. Sin has a willful dimension to it of rebellion against God. It rightly incurs the wrath of God, but for the sake of Christ the redeeming Mediator, God offers "the forgiveness of our trespasses, according to the riches of his grace" (Eph. 1:7). Salvation involves the deliverance from sins, but also, the forgiveness of sin on God's part which makes reconciliation possible: "He has delivered us from the dominion of darkness and transferred us to the kingdom of his beloved Son, in whom we have redemption, the forgiveness of sins" (Col. 1:13-14). Because justification comes through the redeeming blood of Christ, we are saved from the wrath of God (Rom. 5:9).

Paul made this point of forgiveness in comparison to the old covenant in the climax to his sermon in Antioch of Pisidia: "Let it be known to you therefore, brethren, that through this man forgiveness of sins is proclaimed to you, and by him every one that believes is freed from everything from which you could not be freed by the law of Moses" (Acts 13:38-39). Peter concluded his great sermon on the Day of Pentecost with the same offer of forgiveness in the name of Jesus (Acts 2:38). The Lord's Supper symbolizes the forgiveness that God extended to all who would receive redemption as a gracious gift (Rom. 3:24-25a).

*Cleansing*

Christ accomplished what mere animal sacrifice could never do. The sacrifices could not make a change in the nature of people. Regardless of God's willingness to forgive sin, it persisted. The rituals of sacrifice and worship never flattered or enhanced God. He commanded them as a means of instructing Israel on the need for holiness (Gal. 3:24; 4:2-5).

The prophet Amos expressed God's attitude toward the ritual offerings of the nation:

> "I hate, I despise your feasts,
> and I take no delight in your solemn assemblies.
> Even though you offer me your
> burnt offerings and cereal offerings,
> I will not accept them,
> and the peace offerings of your fatted beasts
> I will not look upon.
> Take away from me the noise of your songs;
> to the melody of your harps I will not listen.
> But let justice roll down like waters,
> and righteousness like an everflowing stream" (5:21-24).

The rituals of the old covenant accomplished a ceremonial purification or cleansing, but they did not affect the nature of people. They did not effect a change in character. God gave the new covenant to go beyond what the old covenant had done. Instead of treating the outward form of ceremonial purity, the new covenant attacks the inner problem of spiritual cleansing.

The old covenant forms an analogy for what Christ accomplished in terms of cleansing the inner person:

> For if the sprinkling of defiled persons with the blood of goats and bulls and with the ashes of a heifer sanctifies for the purification of the flesh, how much more shall the blood of Christ, who through the eternal Spirit offered himself without blemish to God, purify your conscience from dead works to serve the living God (Heb. 9:13-14).

The new covenant brings about a spiritual transformation just as God had promised through the prophet Jeremiah. Sin is not simply a legal matter that implies forgiveness or punishment. It is a spiritual problem that implies cleansing or death. The new covenant ratified by the blood of Christ has a permanent and continuing affect for those who abide in Christ. Christ is the unblemished one, and we share His purity to the extent that we abide in Him. He cleanses us by His presence: "If we walk in the light, as he is in the light, we have fellowship with one another, and the blood of Jesus his Son cleanses us from all sin" (1 John 1:7). In the Book of Revelation, the vision of John sees Christ as the Lamb slain whose blood brings cleansing (Rev. 7:14).

## Reconciliation

The old covenant provided for peace offerings. The constant state of sin with its rebellion required a constant effort to make peace with God. Under the old covenant, responsibility lay with the sinner to make the gesture of peace toward God, but under the new covenant, God took the initiative in making peace. From conception to execution, God took the initiative in the redemption of the world. Christ carried out the plan, not as an agent of God, but as God: "For in him all the fullness of God was pleased to dwell, and through him to reconcile to himself all things, whether on earth or in heaven, making peace by the blood of his cross" (Col. 1:19-20). Christ literally accomplished the reconciliation in Himself.

By coming into the world and taking the form of a man, God brought together both His divine self and humanity. Jesus died as Son of God and Son of David. By His redemptive death, Christ extends this reconciliation to the very world that rebelled against God: "You, who once were estranged and hostile in mind, doing evil deeds, he has now reconciled in his body of flesh by his death" (Col. 1:21-22). This reconciliation brings about more than the legal reconciliation that the peace offering brought under the old covenant. The offering brought only a temporary, uneasy peace until sin renewed the rebellion again. But under the new covenant, God makes reconciliation based on the change He makes in people:

> Therefore, if any one is in Christ, he is a new creation; the old has passed away, behold, the new has come. All this is from God, who through Christ reconciled us to himself and gave us the ministry of reconciliation; that is, in Christ God was reconciling the world to him-

self, not counting their trespasses against them, and entrusting to us the message of reconciliation (2 Cor. 5:17-19).

Those who have faith in Christ participate in His life and undergo the transformation that accompanies reconciliation to God. The Lord's Supper symbolizes this participation through the eating and drinking (1 Cor. 10:16).

## Ransom

Freedom, redemption, forgiveness, cleansing, and reconciliation come at a great cost. When the Bible speaks of the ransom, it refers to the cost. Under the law of the old covenant, everything had a value for determining restitution. If someone stole an ox or a sheep and sold it or killed it, he had to restore five oxen for an ox and four sheep for a sheep. If, on the other hand, he had no means to make restitution, he would be sold into slavery. The idea of making things right permeated the law, but how does one make restitution for sin which, despite its physical manifestations, is essentially a spiritual matter? The plight of humanity is that we have no resources for correcting the damage of sin, either to others or to ourselves.

The law expounded a situation in which a man had an ox that had gored someone. The animal had gored in the past, but the man took no steps to confine the animal. Under the law, the animal and the man stood under penalty of death. The law provided for redemption, however: "If a ransom is laid on him, then he shall give for the redemption of his life whatever is laid upon him" (Ex. 21:30). In this case, the ransom referred to the cost of redemption. The death of Christ served to redeem the world from all sin because His life had such surpassing worth to the Father. Because of His dynamic relationship to the Father, Christ can serve as Mediator between God and humans. It cost Him His life to redeem the world, but He freely "gave himself as a ransom for all " (1 Tim. 2:6).

Christ supplied the ransom for those who could not ransom their own lives:

Truly no man can ransom himself,
or give to God the price of his life,
for the ransom of his life is costly,
and can never suffice,

that he could continue to live on for ever,
and never see the Pit (Ps. 49:7-9).

People do not have the spiritual resources to prolong their own lives.
No physical thing of value can affect the eternal life of a person. Some
other source of value had to be introduced to provide everlasting life.
Only the Source of life could alter the quality and nature of human
life.

The futility of the old covenant lay in its inability to alter the quality
and nature of life. Regardless of how well people kept the law, they
could not add enough value to their lives to ransom themselves from
death. Under the new covenant, however, Christ offered His own life
of perfection to infuse those who could not change themselves from
mortal to immortal: "You know that you were ransomed from the
futile ways inherited from your fathers, not with perishable things
such as silver or gold, but with the precious blood of Christ, like that
of a lamb without blemish or spot" (1 Pet. 1:18-19).

The ransom refers to what it cost Christ to change our nature and
our relationship to God. The change involved more than the legal demands of the old covenant; it involved the institution of a new basis for
relationship to God. Under the old covenant, God made His abode in
the holy of holies, but under the new covenant He would abide within
each believer, bringing life and a change in nature that results in the
fruit of the Spirit. Ransomed by God in Christ, we now belong to
Him: "Do you not know that your body is a temple of the Holy Spirit
within you, which you have from God? You are not your own; you
were bought with a price. So glorify God in your body" (1 Cor. 6:19-
20). The new covenant creates a new basis for obedience. Instead of
living righteously to earn the acceptance of God, we are free to live
righteously in gratitude for having been accepted.

*Life Under the New Covenant*

In His life, Christ fulfilled the purpose and meaning of the law. In
His death, He fulfilled the legal demands of the law. He lived and died
trusting the Father for what lay ahead, and this same faith forms the
basis for entry into the new covenant. Faith forms the means of receiving the blessings of the new covenant characterized by the Spirit of
God, rather than the letter of the law. His Spirit alive and at work

within Christians now makes growth and service possible, for "our competence is from God, who has made us competent to be ministers of a new covenant, not in a written code but in the Spirit" (2 Cor. 3:5-6). Thus, the new covenant completes the freedom and salvation of which the old covenant was a foretaste.

Jesus said, "Do this in remembrance of me." The Lord's Supper is a constant reminder of what Christ did to make salvation in all of its dimensions possible. Through remembering with grateful hearts, we abide in Him and draw near to Him. Never taking for granted the blood of the new covenant, we grow by His grace. Paul described the living witness of those being transformed under the new covenant in his second Letter to the Corinthians:

> You yourselves are our letter of recommendation; written on your hearts, to be known and read by all men; and you show that you are a letter from Christ delivered by us, written not with ink but with the Spirit of the living God, not on tablets of stone but on tablets of human hearts (2 Cor. 3:2-3).

And against such there is no law.

# 13 ||| The New Birth

In Galatians, Paul contrasts the fruit of the Spirit and the work of the flesh. The passions and desires of the flesh stand in opposition to the desires of the Spirit of God. The desires of the flesh prevent the fruit of the Spirit from appearing. While the law could not prevent this sin condition, Christ made it possible for people to have victory over sin. Paul says, "those who belong to Christ Jesus have crucified the flesh with its passions and desires" (Gal. 5:24).

Baptism symbolizes this death of the flesh and the subsequent new life that results from belonging to Christ and being possessed by His Holy Spirit. While the Lord's Supper describes how Christ accomplished salvation, baptism describes how the Holy Spirit applies salvation to those who believe. The Lord's Supper describes how Christ settled the problem of sin and made peace with God, but baptism describes how His sacrifice affects us. While the Lord's Supper focuses on the change in legal standing with God as a result of the law by Christ, baptism focuses on the change in our relationship with God as a result of a spiritual transformation brought about by the Holy Spirit. The Lord's Supper focuses on justification, and baptism focuses on regeneration. The Lord's Supper describes how God sent away the bad: sin and death. Baptism describes how God brought in the good: eternal life.

## Crucified with Christ

Christ's death makes salvation possible only for those who have faith in Him. Baptism served as one's profession of faith in the early church and symbolically represents what Christians believe has happened to them because of the death and resurrection of Christ. Paul explained the meaning of baptism to the Romans:

> Do you not know that all of us who have been baptized into Christ Jesus were baptized into his death? We were buried therefore with him by baptism into death, so that as Christ was raised from the dead by the glory of the Father, we too might walk in newness of life (Rom. 6:3-4).

In baptism, Christians dramatically act out what has spiritually happened to them. They have united themselves with the death of Christ. They have also united themselves with "the power of his resurrection" (Phil. 3:10).

Union with Christ applies His substitutionary death to the believer. The benefit of Christ's death takes effect when one is united with Him through faith. Baptism symbolizes this union. Christ died for all who unite themselves with His death through faith. When we have faith, not only the substitution occurs but also a transference: I die in Christ's death, He lives in my flesh. As Paul explained, "I have been crucified with Christ; it is no longer I who live, but Christ who lives in me; and the life I now live in the flesh I live by faith in the Son of God, who loved me and gave himself for me" (Gal. 2:20). Baptism symbolizes the Christian's faith that his or her guilt and sin nature died with Christ on the cross. He bore my sins and guilt because by faith in Him, I died with Him.

Salvation requires this union and identification with Christ which Paul described as being "in Christ" (Eph. 1:3). The Lord Himself on the night He was betrayed described this saving relationship as abiding in Him. Christ has already experienced death for those who abide in Him. In retrospect, those who abide in Christ have already died with respect to sin and the domination of evil over their lives. Peter said of this experience, "He himself bore our sins in his body on the tree, that we might die to sin and live to righteousness" (1 Pet. 2:24). Paul also remarked, "If with Christ you died to the elemental spirits of the universe, why do you live as if you still belonged to the world?" (Col. 2:20).

In salvation, the old self with its guilt and domination by the world order dies. United with Christ in His death, the believer experiences the transformation of His resurrection. Baptism represents this death of the old self, for the "old self was crucified with him so that the sinful body might be destroyed" (Rom. 6:6). Baptism also represents the creation of a transformed life resurrected from the body of death:

"Therefore, if any one is in Christ, he is a new creation; the old has passed away, behold, the new has come" (2 Cor. 5:17). Both in death and resurrection, the essential qualification for these to affect one's salvation is that one experience them "in Christ." A reflexive substitution must take place in order for Christ to bear our sins and us to bear His life.

Paul clearly described the symbolism of baptism in his Letter to the Colossians. The visual image of baptism focuses on the burial of a dead person. Brought to the grave, the body is lowered into the ground. In baptism, believers are lowered under the water as though entombed. Here they publicly declare that they have shared the death and burial of Jesus who was placed in the tomb. As Christ rose from the dead, however, believers also rise out of the water as testimony of their faith that they share the resurrection of Christ (Col. 2:12-15).

Unless one shares the death of Christ, one cannot share the resurrection of Christ. By uniting in His death, we are reconciled to God in Him who carried our sins to the grave. Unless our sins die with Him as we die with Him, we must bear our own sins. If we do not share His resurrection, we have no power over the tomb. One can hardly rise from the dead with Him if one has not died with Him. This spiritual death and resurrection occur as one unites with Christ through faith. Through this process one puts on Christ (Gal. 3:27) and puts off the body of flesh (Col. 2:11). As a result, Christians should consider themselves "dead to sin and alive to God in Christ Jesus" (Rom. 6:11).

This reflexive substitution has profound implications for living the Christian life and bearing spiritual fruit. Holy living depends upon knowing that one has died to sin and to the control that sin has over human nature. Holy living depends upon knowing that one has experienced the life-changing power of the resurrection, and this means a new capacity for victory over the temptation and domination of sin. Holy living depends upon "always carrying in the body the death of Jesus, so that the life of Jesus may also be manifested in our bodies. For while we live we are always being given up to death for Jesus' sake, so that the life of Jesus may be manifested in our mortal flesh" (2 Cor. 4:10). Holy living depends upon the manifestation of Christ in our lives.

Baptism pictures this experience and dramatically portrays why the death and resurrection of Jesus two thousand years ago have significance for someone living today. Baptism in and of itself has no saving significance, but as a vivid enactment of one's experience with Christ, it serves as a point of reference in Christian spiritual life that recalls what happened when one first turned to Christ in faith. Baptism represents one's reliance on Christ through death to life. Rather than corresponding to the washing away of sin, baptism corresponds to the appeal of faith in God: "Baptism, which corresponds to this, now saves you, not as a removal of dirt from the body but as an appeal to God for a clear conscience, through the resurrection of Jesus Christ" (1 Pet. 3:21). The act of baptism proclaims a new Christian's faith in Jesus Christ, the Son of God, who died for our sins, was dead and buried, and who rose again from the dead (1 Cor. 15:3-4). Baptism expresses this essential kernel of the gospel with the conviction that we too may be "raised with him through faith in the working of God" (Col. 2:12).

### Born of the Spirit

In explaining the reflexive character of salvation, Christ declared, "Abide in me, and I in you" (John 15:4). While death to sin occurs as one abides in Christ, eternal life comes through Christ abiding in us. God does not give eternal life as a commodity that one might possess or hold title to. Rather than a possession, eternal life refers to the condition of being possessed by God. Eternal life depends upon belonging to God, and it happens when God takes possession of someone who desires to belong to God.

Christians obtain more than immortality, they obtain Christ, the Source of life: "This is the testimony, that God gave us eternal life, and this life is in his Son. He who has the Son has life; he who has not the Son of God has not life" (1 John 5:11-12). Those who pursue life miss it, but those who pursue Christ gain life as the by-product. Paul considered all of the reasons for religious confidence to be of no value and gave up everything that he might "gain Christ and be found in him" (Phil. 3:8-9). Christ Himself is the goal and the prize. Those who abide in Him find that He abides in them.

Christ abides in believers through His Holy Spirit. The Holy Spirit brings eternal life by virtue of His presence. Eternal life results from someone receiving the gift of the presence of the Holy Spirit. God's presence is the sign that He has forgiven sin and restored the relationship He intended to have with people before creation. The Holy Spirit brings into believer's life the salvation that Christ made possible: "If the Spirit of him who raised Jesus from the dead dwells in you, he who raised Christ Jesus from the dead will give life to your mortal bodies also through his Spirit which dwells in you" (Rom. 8:11). Baptism depicts this giving of life or regeneration that the Spirit accomplishes.

Jesus explained the necessity of regeneration to Nicodemus in the third chapter of John. The conversation has a rather abrupt beginning. Nicodemus saluted Jesus as a great teacher of the law who had come from God as the miracles He performed bore witness. Jesus responded with a statement that does not seem to follow. As though He had not heard what Nicodemus said, or perhaps as though His mind was wandering, Jesus replied, "Truly, truly, I say to you, unless one is born anew, he cannot see the kingdom of God" (John 3:3). The disjunction between the two greetings may be disturbing, unless one recognizes what Jesus was doing.

Nicodemus knew the law well as a leader among the Pharisees and a member of the Sanhedrin court. While Nicodemus wanted to deal with the law, Jesus immediately challenged every presupposition Nicodemus had about righteousness and admission to the kingdom of God. Rather than being drawn into another lengthy conversation about the right way to do religion, Jesus immediately penetrated to the essential problem of the human race and why its attempts at morality always lead to failure. The nature of people prohibits them from fulfilling their own view of righteousness, much less God's view. They have to be changed in their nature. They have to be born again.

In the next chapter, Jesus used the same rhetorical approach when talking with the woman at the well. She raised the question of religious observance. Her ancestors had worshiped on the mountain in Samaria for centuries, but her distant relatives, the Jews, worshiped on the mountain in Jerusalem. She wanted to know which was the right place. Jesus did not answer her question, just as He had not responded to the agenda of Nicodemus. Instead, He challenged her understanding of the meaning of worship:

> "You worship what you do not know; we worship what we know, for salvation is from the Jews. But the hour is coming, and now is, when the true worshipers will worship the Father in spirit and truth, for such

the Father seeks to worship him. God is spirit, and those who worship
him must worship in spirit and truth" (John 4:22-24).

A fundamental change must occur in the nature of people before even
true worship can happen. People must have a basis for acting in a
spiritual way, rather than a fleshly way.

In pursuing the matter with Nicodemus, Jesus stressed the distinction between flesh and spirit. In their natural state, people cannot experience the spiritual kingdom. They cannot enter it or exist in it for
"that which is born of flesh is flesh, and that which is born of Spirit is
spirit" (John 3:6). This dramatic distinction between flesh and spirit
serves as a haunting reminder of the plight of humanity: "You are
dust, and to dust you shall return" (Gen. 3:19). The radical separation
of the sinfulness of people, referred to as the "flesh," and the holiness
of God, the Spirit, appeared in the encounter between God and Moses.
Moses desired to see the glory of the Lord, but the Lord told him,
"You cannot see my face; for man shall not see me and live" (Ex.
33:20).

The fact that God went to some pains to allow Moses a glimpse of
His afterglow demonstrates that God meant no malice toward Moses.
He did not say, "If you look at me, I will kill you." He simply in-
formed Moses of the reality of the curse of sin which forms a barrier
between humans and God. Sin cannot exist in the presence of the holiness of God. Some have mistakenly paraphrased God's exchange with
Moses to read, "God cannot look upon sin." Actually, God can do
anything He wants to do. The problem lies with us. We cannot behold
Him. To behold His glory in a sinful state would be like the morning
mist that vaporizes in the light of the morning sun. Sin is not just a
legal problem that must be set right; it is a problem of the nature of the
human spirit that must be changed.

Jesus explained that this radical change in nature is like being "born
again" or, as a literal translation of the Greek would read, "born from
above." This birth comes through the agency of the Holy Spirit from
above. Jesus used water as a metaphor for the Holy Spirit, and baptism symbolically represents the transformation that occurs when
someone experiences the new birth through the Holy Spirit. In explaining the new birth as the prerequisite for entrance into the kingdom, Jesus said, "Unless one is born of water and the Spirit, he cannot

enter the kingdom of God" (John 3:5). In verses 6 and 8, however, Jesus did not mention water and only spoke of being born of the Spirit.

The reference to water seems to be in the form of Hebrew parallelism whereby a prophet said the same thing in two ways. An example from the Psalms would be: "Create in me a clean heart, O God; and renew a right spirit within me (51:10, KJV). Both lines say the same thing, and "heart" serves as a metaphor for "spirit." This seems to be the way Jesus used water with spirit. He used the same meaning in several other places in the Gospel of John.

In the fourth chapter of John when Jesus engaged the Samaritan woman in conversation beside Jacob's well, He used water to speak of the Holy Spirit as the source of regeneration. He told her: "Whoever drinks of the water that I shall give him will never thirst; the water that I shall give him will become in him a spring of water welling up to eternal life" (John 4:14). Later in John, Jesus carried the metaphor further, and this time John gave the specific explanation of what was meant by water:

> "If any one thirst, let him come to me and drink. He who believes in me, as the scripture has said, 'Out of his heart shall flow rivers of living water.' " Now this he said about the Spirit, which those who believed in him were to receive (John 7:37-39).

As a final clue to understanding the symbolic relationship between water and the Spirit in John's Gospel, consider how John the Baptist used the words in the first chapter. John said that he came baptizing with water (John 1:26,31,33), but One was coming who would baptize with the Holy Spirit (John 1:33). Water baptism by immersion symbolically represents the baptism of the Holy Spirit whereby God regenerates a believer.

### The Baptism of the Holy Spirit

The use of water to describe the regeneration that comes by the Spirit has its roots in the Old Testament. The baptism of the Holy Spirit fulfills prophecy. In the early part of the Old Testament, the Spirit of God is spoken of in terms of wind or breath. During the time of the prophets, however, God began to reveal the Spirit as bringing life and refreshment, like water in a desert. Isaiah prophesied:

> "For I will pour water on the thirsty land,

and streams on the dry ground;
I will pour my Spirit upon your descendants,
and my blessing on your offspring" (Isa. 44:3).

Ezekiel spoke of the Spirit as a river that flowed from the temple of God which could make the Dead Sea swarm with life, and "everything will live where the river goes" (47:9). Jeremiah spoke of God as the "fountain of living waters" (2:13; 17:13). Joel prophesied about the last days: "It shall come to pass," God declared, "that I will pour out my spirit on all flesh" (2:28). On the Day of Pentecost when the Holy Spirit fell upon the church, Peter cited this passage from Joel to explain to the people what had happened. Prophecy was fulfilled.

The baptism of the Spirit is not a subsequent second blessing after salvation, as some have argued. Apart from this experience of the Spirit a person does not belong to Christ. Viewing salvation as only a legal matter has probably led to the error that people can be saved without the Holy Spirit taking possession of them. On the contrary, Scripture asserts, "Any one who does not have the Spirit of Christ does not belong to him" (Rom. 8:9). This error has also led to an emphasis on ecstatic gifts rather than fruit as a sign of one's relationship to Christ and of one 's maturity in the faith. This misplaced emphasis seems odd since gifts can be imitated, but fruit cannot be. While every Christian is gifted in some way by the Holy Spirit, only the mature in the faith produce much fruit.

## Conclusion

Baptism represents symbolically how Christians have died to sin in Christ, how they have risen with Christ from the tomb, and how they have been born from above by the Holy Spirit. As water symbolically represents the Holy Spirit, baptism by immersion in water dramatically portrays their faith that God has engulfed them in His Spirit. Baptism serves as a way of proclaiming the message of the gospel because it portrays the death, burial, and resurrection of the Lord as well as His gift of life through the Holy Spirit to those who have faith in Him.

Baptism is meant to occur once for a Christian because one's death to sin and rebirth through the Holy Spirit occur only once. Because the new birth has happened, however, baptism supplies a source of comfort and reminds Christians that they have a reason for hope and a basis for spiritual growth. Baptism reminds Christian's that the Spirit of God dwells within them and that they now belong to Christ. Because baptism also represents the new birth, it reminds Christians that they begin salvation as babes in Christ. Baptism itself reminds Christians that they must grow to maturity in Christ.

Without an understanding that salvation involves more than one's legal standing with respect to sin, a Christian has no real basis for growing in the faith. If salvation only means forgiveness of sins, then sanctification with its growth in holiness has no basis. On the Day of Pentecost when Peter preached the first gospel sermon, however, he made the point clearly that salvation also involves the indwelling of the Holy Spirit who applies the forgiveness and changes the nature of the people Christ has justified: "Repent, and be baptized every one of you in the name of Jesus Christ for the forgiveness of your sins; and you shall receive the gift of the Holy Spirit" (Acts 2:38). Because we have been crucified with Christ and have risen with Him to walk in newness of life, the flesh no longer has the same power over us. *Flesh,* one should note, does not refer to one's physical nature but to one's sinful nature. God created the physical body good. *The flesh* refers to the corruption of the human nature, but Paul reminds us that "you are not in the flesh, you are in the Spirit, if in fact the Spirit of God dwells in you" (Rom. 8:9).

Baptism represents what has happened to release a Christian from the corruption of sin. Obedience to the law does not create the change. Rather, the change now makes obedience to God a possibility. Because "those who belong to Christ Jesus have crucified the flesh with its passions and desires" (Gal. 5:24), Scripture instructs us, "Let not sin therefore reign in your mortal bodies, to make you obey their passions" (Rom. 6:12). He has recreated us to grow a different way.

# 14 ||| From Glory Unto Glory

A man in his mid-twenties had struggled with his spiritual life for years before he came to me for help. He had tried to be a good Christian, but he had failed utterly. He stood at the point of despair, prepared to give up the church for good. As we talked, he affirmed his strong belief in the existence of God and spoke of his conviction that he had witnessed powerful demonstrations of God's miraculous workings. However, he had reached a point where he did not care anymore. While the man continued to describe his religious experience, I realized that he had talked for fifteen minutes without mentioning Christ. He had no Savior. Instead, he struggled in his own strength to become righteous and acceptable to God. His efforts only convinced him of his utter unworthiness.

In that moment I gained a deeper understanding than I had ever known of the desperate necessity of a Savior. That man needed to be saved from the power of sin and death. Powerless to deal with his own failure, he needed someone to extricate him from his rendezvous with destruction. He had been laboring for years under conviction of sin, trying to be righteous out of guilt, shame, and a belief that he ought to be different. Yet, the man had never taken the crucial step that would begin the transformation of his life. He had never entrusted his life to Jesus Christ. He had never trusted Christ to bring him to the Father free from sin. He had never had faith in Christ to save him until that morning.

Before my eyes, I saw a physical change in that man as the grace of God enveloped him. As he opened his heart to Christ, the highly agitated and disturbed face that had wept in despair melted into a peaceful glow. Christ had begun a work in him, the end of which is yet to be revealed. Until Christ began it, however, nothing good could happen.

The fruit could not begin to appear until Christ lived within him to produce it. Neither can fruit continue to appear and flourish in abundance unless a Christian abides in Christ.

## Knowing the Savior

Christ is literally the beginning and the end of a Christian's life. He is the alpha and omega of existence. He is not the means to life; He is life (John 14:6). He came into this world to share His life that we might be changed. The forgiveness of sin and the gift of the Holy Spirit are only the beginning of this new life. Beyond this first work of grace, Jesus intends so much more for those who love Him. "And we all, with unveiled face, beholding the glory of the Lord, are being changed into his likeness from one degree of glory to another; for this comes from the Lord who is the Spirit" (2 Cor. 3:18). No method, technique, or discipline can bring about this change apart from Christ.

One of the technological marvels of this age is the banking machine. Once upon a time, when a person forgot to cash a check at the bank before it closed, one went without money. Now, anyone who has a bank card can withdraw money from a banking machine at any hour of the day or night. Before the procedure will work, however, a person has to know a personal access number. Without the access number, it matters not how much money we have in the bank; we cannot reach it. In the same manner, Christ is our only access to the qualities of holiness that satisfy the cravings of life. He said, "Apart from me you can do nothing" (John 15:5).

Receiving the benefits of Christ, however, is not exactly like taking money out of a bank. In another sense, it is like a cold winter morning in an old house. The wooden boards of the floor are icy cold. The chilling draft whistles through the window sill. Even the woolen clothes you have just put on are freezing to the touch. Then you go into the living room where your father has built a fire in the wood stove. As you draw near, you become warm. Soon the misery of the cold is forgotten. You are warm because of your nearness to the source of heat. You are warm because of the warmth. You are not warm in the same way the stove is. It generates warmth, but you enjoy the benefit of its warmth.

We partake of the life of Christ in our relationship to Him. We share the holiness of Christ in our nearness to Him. We benefit from

His grace as we are willing to receive it and be affected by it.

I remember one Christmastime. Like Abraham and Sarah, Mary Anne and I had moved, and we were going to have a baby. I had accepted a ministerial responsibility I never considered as an option or a possibility. I had accepted a call to serve as a denominational executive charged with the responsibility of evangelism. During that Christmastime, we visited churches and Sunday School classes to find a spiritual home.

In one Sunday School class, the leader asked people to share what Christmas meant to them. One man set a negative tone by railing against the commercialism of Christmas. When Christians are supposed to stand for peace, children want toys that support violent fantasies. He then proceeded to list a catalog of social ills that society ignores while Christmas is promoted as a major business.

He made the point that the church needed to be more aggressive in confronting society and the sources of injustice. He cringed at the expressions of piety by Christians when the needs of the world are so great. Yet, with all of this on the man's mind, frustration overcame him at the point of knowing what to do. Having condemned everyone else for the sad state of the world, it became evident that he was not doing anything about any of the ills.

I have always stood in utter amazement at Christians who are frustrated by the wickedness of the world. Christmas is the biggest merchandising festival of the year. It is the grandest marketing extravaganza ever conceived. It is a time for indulging the greed, lusts, and whims of the flesh. How foolish to expect anything else! To keep Christmas, one must have Christ. The things that Christ taught are utter foolishness unless Christ is the Lord, "For the word of the cross is folly to those who are perishing" (1 Cor. 1:18). If Christ is not the Lord, then the Epicureans are right: Let us eat, drink, and be merry, for tomorrow we die.

Sadly, the Sunday School member and most of the others in the class had lost the meaning of Christmas. Impassioned as he was, he had a cold intellectual religion that consisted of rules of behavior and social responsibility. He saw no point in proclaiming Christ when there were things to do. Thus, he chose to withhold from the world the only thing that would make the world different. He chose to withhold the Savior while condemning the world for not being Christlike.

He had forgotten what it means to be lost. The world still needs a Savior. All the people who subvert justice still need a Savior. All the people who oppress the poor still need a Savior. All the victims still need a Savior. And until they have a Savior, they will not change.

More sadly, he had forgotten what it meant to be saved. He lived in his own strength and power. At some time in the man's life, the proclamation of Christ had been so important that he accepted the teachings of the Savior. In the process of time, however, the Savior had become superfluous. Thus, he sat frustrated by his impotence to do anything. Instead of the fruit of the Spirit, his life showed anger, hostility, frustration, cynicism, and despair. Piety, or the daily wonder that comes from conversation with the Lord and meditation on His profound goodness and mercy, received his ridicule.

In contrast to this angry Christian, Jesus never focused anger or frustration on the sinners who caused the problems of society. He wept over the Jerusalem that would crucify Him. He loved the rich young ruler who chose wealth over the kingdom of God. He had compassion on the ignorant multitudes, as well as on the sick and lame. Jesus only vented His anger against the religious community that did not take prayer and piety seriously. In His only outburst, He cleared the temple of those who had lost their sense of awe in the presence of God. The merchants practiced a form of godliness but denied the power thereof.

This unfortunate man was right to want to see the world a better place. He was right to want people to do the right thing. The tragedy of his spiritual immaturity rested in his failure to recognize that the ability and the possibility of doing the right thing only comes from the Lord. The man's own failure, even when he wanted to do something significant, points up the fact that not only the power but the motivation must come from the Lord. When the fruit of the Spirit ripens in the lives of Christians, they do the works of their Father.

## Being Like the Father

Most families have some physical characteristic that carries over from generation to generation. The Poes have had prominent foreheads and noses for generations. I have the same forehead as my cousin Edgar Allan. Because of the genes that come from my parents, I inherit certain characteristics. The genes that determine the basic characteristics that I brought into this life are a power at work within me. Sometimes when people say that I am like my father or my mother, they mean I have my father's forehead and nose or my mother's eyes and smile. The genes I inherited from my parents determine these things.

Sometimes when people say that I am like my father, however, they mean something entirely different. My wife tells me that many of my mannerisms remind her of my father. I have noticed one in particular. My father is a gentleman in the noblest sense of the word. When he is introduced to a lady, he salutes her with a courtly bow so gracefully and naturally executed that it seems the normal thing to do even in the ebbing years of the twentieth century. At some point a few years ago, I noticed that I have my father's bow. I do not know how or when I began to do it, but it has become a natural part of me.

Part of being like my father comes from genes, but part of it comes from being with my father. From spending time with him and, I suppose, wanting to be like him, I became like him. The closeness of our relationship led to my adopting many of his ways. Jesus said that the context for becoming like Him rests in the closeness of our relationship to Him "Take my yoke upon you, and learn from me; for I am gentle and lowly in heart, and you will find rest for your souls. For my yoke is easy, and my burden is light" (Matt. 11:29-30). The qualities of the fruit of the Spirit have no meaning by themselves. They do not exist as realities apart from Christ. We learn from Him what they really are.

Because of His Holy Spirit in us, we have a power at work which makes us like our Heavenly Father, much the same as genes transfer the traits from one generation to the next. Being a child of God includes sharing the qualities of the Father. Eternal life is one of these. Holiness is another. For this reason, the New Testament speaks of Christians as saints or "holy ones." The Holy Spirit reproduces the holy character of God in His adoptive children. Paul called the characteristics of this holiness the fruit of the Spirit in Galatians 5:22-23. The fruit of the Spirit characterizes what we are, and what we are makes possible what we do.

Just as the Holy Spirit produces the fruit of holiness in a child of God, the children of God produce fruit unto God in their deeds. The fruit of the Spirit is internal, while the fruit of a Christian life consists in the external things we do. As children of God, God expects Christians to do His will as well as exhibit His character. Jesus said, "We must work the works of him who sent me, while it is day; night comes, when no one can work" (John 9:4). Eternal life is one implication of being a child of God. Doing the will of the Father is another.

In spending time with my earthly father and desiring to be like him, I began to do things the way he does them. In spending time with our Lord and desiring to be like Him, we begin to do things the way He would do them. Doing His will does not come so much in having a prescribed list of obligations to fulfill as it comes in knowing the mind of Jesus. Bearing the fruit of the Spirit and doing the will of the Father does not come from pursuing these goals. Rather, the fruit comes from seeking Christ.

Peace, like the other qualities of holiness, is not a static gift that a Christian can save or stockpile. We only have access to the gift through Christ. In fact, He is the gift; the rest is a by-product of His presence. Paul did not say that Christ gives peace. He said that Christ "is our peace" (Eph. 2:14). Christ did not promise to give His disciples peace; instead, He promised them *His* peace (John 14:27). The gift is indistinguishable from the Giver. Christ must dwell richly in a heart for that heart to have the fruit of His Spirit. People cannot lay hold of love, joy, peace, or any other dimension of holiness. We can only lay hold of Christ.

The poor human race has always confused desire and fulfillment. We desire love and every other condition which makes for happiness as an end in itself. Instead, we ought to seek out the Source of all happiness and the object of fulfillment. The experience of the fruit of the Spirit rests in the final apprehension by the heart, as well as the mind, that Christ is the end of all desire. All goodness wells from Him, as the old hymn pleads, "Come, thou Fount of ev'ry blessing." Blessings can no more be stored up than sunshine. The fulfillment of all human longing, the quenching of spiritual thirst, comes as a steady stream. Jesus called it a "spring of water welling up to eternal life" (John 4:14). Apart from the stream, the heart's true cravings and needs cannot be met.

Having the blessing does not come from seeking the blessing, but from seeking Christ and abiding in Him. All His riches in glory are already ours in Him. But only in Him are they ours.